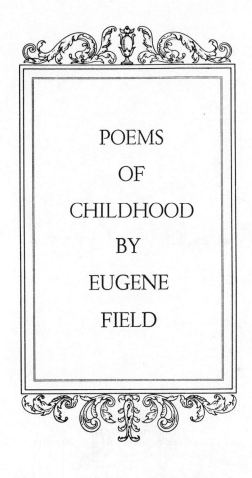

POEMS
OF
CHILDHOOD
BY
EUGENE
FIELD

Illustrated by MARY NORTON

AVENEL BOOKS
A DIVISION OF CROWN PUBLISHERS, INC.
NEW YORK

WITH TRUMPET AND DRUM

WITH big tin trumpet and little red drum,
    Marching like soldiers, the children come!
It's this way and that way they circle and file—
    My! but that music of theirs is fine!
This way and that way, and after a while
    They march straight into this heart of mine!
A sturdy old heart, but it has to succumb
To the blare of that trumpet and beat of that drum!

Come on, little people, from cot and from hall—
This heart it hath welcome and room for you all!
    It will sing you its songs and warm you with love,
        As your dear little arms with my arms intertwine;
    It will rock you away to the dreamland above—
        Oh, a jolly old heart is this old heart of mine,
And jollier still is it bound to become
When you blow that big trumpet and beat that red drum!

So come; though I see not *his* dear little face
And hear not *his* voice in this jubilant place,
    I know he were happy to bid me enshrine
        His memory deep in my heart with your play—
    Ah me! but a love that is sweeter than mine
        Holdeth my boy in its keeping to-day!
And my heart it is lonely—so, little folk, come,
March in and make merry with trumpet and drum!

KRINKEN

KRINKEN was a little child,—
    It was summer when he smiled.
Oft the hoary sea and grim
Stretched its white arms out to him,
Calling, "Sun-child, come to me;

Let me warm my heart with thee!"
But the child heard not the sea.

Krinken on the beach one day
Saw a maiden Nis at play;
Fair, and very fair, was she,
Just a little child was he.
"Krinken," said the maiden Nis,
"Let me have a little kiss,—
Just a kiss, and go with me
To the summer-lands that be
Down within the silver sea."
Krinken was a little child,
By the maiden Nis beguiled;
Down into the calling sea
With the maiden Nis went he.
But the sea calls out no more;
It is winter on the shore,—
Winter where that little child
Made sweet summer when he smiled:
Though 'tis summer on the sea
Where with maiden Nis went he,—
Summer, summer evermore,—
It is winter on the shore,
Winter, winter evermore.

Of the summer on the deep
Come sweet visions in my sleep;
His fair face lifts from the sea,
His dear voice calls out to me,—
These my dreams of summer be.

Krinken was a little child,
By the maiden Nis beguiled;
Oft the hoary sea and grim
Reached its longing arms to him,
Crying, "Sun-child, come to me;

Let me warm my heart with thee!"
But the sea calls out no more;
It is winter on the shore,—
Winter, cold and dark and wild;
Krinken was a little child,—
It was summer when he smiled;
Down he went into the sea,
And the winter bides with me.
Just a little child was he.

THE NAUGHTY DOLL

MY dolly is a dreadful care,—
   Her name is Miss Amandy;
I dress her up and curl her hair,
   And feed her taffy candy.
Yet heedless of the pleading voice
   Of her devoted mother,
She will not wed her mother's choice,
   But says she'll wed another.

I'd have her wed the china vase,—
   There is no Dresden rarer;
You might go searching every place
   And never find a fairer.
He is a gentle, pinkish youth,—
   Of that there's no denying;
Yet when I speak of him, forsooth,
   Amandy falls to crying!

She loves the drum—that's very plain—
   And scorns the vase so clever;
And weeping, vows she will remain
   A spinster doll forever!
The protestations of the drum
   I am convinced are hollow:

3

When once distressing times should come,
    How soon would ruin follow!

Yet all in vain the Dresden boy
    From yonder mantel woos her;
A mania for that vulgar toy,
    The noisy drum, imbues her!
In vain I wheel her to and fro,
    And reason with her mildly,—
Her waxen tears in torrents flow,
    Her sawdust heart beats wildly.

I'm sure that when I'm big and tall,
    And wear long trailing dresses,
I sha'n't encourage beaux at all
    Till mama acquiesces;
Our choice will be a suitor then
    As pretty as this vase is,—
Oh, how we'll hate the noisy men
    With whiskers on their faces!

NIGHTFALL IN DORDRECHT

THE mill goes toiling slowly around
        With steady and solemn creak,
And my little one hears in the kindly sound
    The voice of the old mill speak.
While round and round those big white wings
    Grimly and ghostlike creep,
My little one hears that the old mill sings:
    "Sleep, little tulip, sleep!"

The sails are reefed and the nets are drawn,
    And, over his pot of beer,
The fisher, against the morrow's dawn,
    Lustily maketh cheer;
He mocks at the winds that caper along

From the far-off clamorous deep—
But we—we love their lullaby song
    Of "Sleep, little tulip, sleep!"

Old dog Fritz in slumber sound
    Groans of the stony mart—
To-morrow how proudly he'll trot you round,
    Hitched to our new milk-cart!
And you shall help me blanket the kine
    And fold the gentle sheep
And set the herring a-soak in brine—
    But now, little tulip, sleep!

A Dream-One comes to button the eyes
    That wearily droop and blink,
While the old mill buffets the frowning skies
    And scolds at the stars that wink;
Over your face the misty wings
    Of that beautiful Dream-One sweep,
And rocking your cradle she softly sings:
    "Sleep, little tulip, sleep!"

INTRY-MINTRY

WILLIE and Bess, Georgie and May—
    Once, as these children were hard at play
And old man, hoary and tottering, came
And watched them playing their pretty game.
  He seemed to wonder, while standing there,
    What the meaning thereof could be—

Aha, but the old man yearned to share
  Of the little children's innocent glee
As they circled around with laugh and shout
And told their rime at counting out:
    "Intry-mintry, cutrey-corn,
    Apple-seed and apple-thorn;
    Wire, brier, limber, lock,
    Twelve geese in a flock;
    Some flew east, some flew west,
    Some flew over the cuckoo's nest!"

Willie and Bess, Georgie and May—
Ah, the mirth of that summer-day!
'Twas Father Time who had come to share
The innocent joy of those children there;
  He learned betimes the game they played
    And into their sport with them went he—
  How *could* the children have been afraid,
    Since little they recked who he might be?
They laughed to hear old Father Time
Mumbling that curious nonsense rime
    Of "Intry-mintry, cutrey-corn,
    Apple-seed and apple-thorn;
    Wire, brier, limber, lock,
    Twelve geese in a flock;
    Some flew east, some flew west,
    Some flew over the cuckoo's nest!"

Willie and Bess, Georgie and May,
And joy of summer—where are they?
The grim old man still standeth near
Crooning the song of a far-off year;
  And into the winter I come alone,
    Cheered by that mournful requiem,
  Soothed by the dolorous monotone
    That shall count me off as it counted them—
The solemn voice of old Father Time

Chanting the homely nursery rime
He learned of the children a summer morn
When, with "apple-seed and apple-thorn,"
Life was full of the dulcet cheer
That bringeth the grace of heaven anear—
The sound of the little ones hard at play—
Willie and Bess, Georgie and May.

PITTYPAT AND TIPPYTOE

ALL day long they come and go—
Pittypat and Tippytoe;
Footprints up and down the hall,
Playthings scattered on the floor,
Finger-marks along the wall,
Tell-tale smudges on the door—
By these presents you shall know
Pittypat and Tippytoe.

How they riot at their play!
And a dozen times a day
In they troop, demanding bread—
Only buttered bread will do,
And that butter must be spread
Inches thick with sugar too!
And I never can say, "No,
Pittypat and Tippytoe!"

Sometimes there are griefs to soothe,
Sometimes ruffled brows to smooth;
For (I much regret to say)

Tippytoe and Pittypat
Sometimes interrupt their play
With an internecine spat;
Fie, for shame! to quarrel so—
Pittypat and Tippytoe!

Oh, the thousand worrying things
Every day recurrent brings!
Hands to scrub and hair to brush,
Search for playthings gone amiss,
Many a wee complaint to hush,
Many a little bump to kiss;
Life seems one vain, fleeting show
To Pittypat and Tippytoe!

And when day is at an end,
There are little duds to mend:
Little frocks are strangely torn,
Little shoes great holes reveal,
Little hose, but one day worn,
Rudely yawn at toe and heel!
Who but *you* could work such woe,
Pittypat and Tippytoe?

But when comes this thought to me:
"Some there are that childless be,"
Stealing to their little beds,
With a love I cannot speak,
Tenderly I stroke their heads—
Fondly kiss each velvet cheek.
God help those who do not know
A Pittypat or Tippytoe!

On the floor and down the hall,
Rudely smutched upon the wall,
There are proofs in every kind
Of the havoc they have wrought,

And upon my heart you'd find
    Just such trade-marks, if you sought;
Oh, how glad I am 'tis so,
Pittypat and Tippytoe!

BALOW, MY BONNIE

HUSH, bonnie, dinna greit;
    Moder will rocke her sweete,—
      Balow, my boy!
When that his toile ben done,
Daddie will come anone,—
Hush thee, my lyttel one;
      Balow, my boy!

Gin thou dost sleepe, perchaunce
Fayries will come to daunce,—
      Balow, my boy!
Oft hath thy moder seene
Moonlight and mirkland queene
Daunce on thy slumbering een,—
      Balow, my boy!

Then droned a bomblebee
Saftly this songe to thee:
      "Balow, my boy!"
And a wee heather bell,
Pluckt from a fayry dell,
Chimed thee this rune hersell:
      "Balow, my boy!"

Soe, bonnie, dinna greit;
Moder doth rock her sweete,—
    Balow, my boy!
Give mee thy lyttel hand,
Moder will hold it and
Lead thee to balow land,—
    Balow, my boy!

THE HAWTHORNE CHILDREN

THE Hawthorne children—seven in all—
        Are famous friends of mine,
And with what pleasure I recall
How, years ago, one gloomy fall,
        I took a tedious railway line
And journeyed by slow stages down
Unto that sleepy seaport town
        (Albeit one worth seeing),
    Where Hildegarde, John, Henry, Fred,
And Beatrix and Gwendolen
And she that was the baby then—
        These famous seven, as aforesaid,
            Lived, moved, and had their being.

The Hawthorne children gave me such
        A welcome by the sea,
That the eight of us were soon in touch,
And though their mother marvelled much,
        Happy as larks were we!
Egad I was a boy again
With Henry, John, and Gwendolen!
        And, oh! the funny capers
    I cut with Hildegarde and Fred!
The pranks we heedless children played,

The deafening, awful noise we made—
  'Twould shock my family, if they read
    About it in the papers!

The Hawthorne children all were smart;
    The girls, as I recall,
Had comprehended every art
Appealing to the head and heart,
    The boys were gifted, all;
'Twas Hildegarde who showed me how
To hitch the horse and milk a cow
    And cook the best of suppers;
  With Beatrix upon the sands
I sprinted daily, and was beat,
While Henry stumped me to the feat
  Of walking round upon my hands
    Instead of on my "uppers."

The Hawthorne children liked me best
    Of evenings, after tea;
For then, by general request,
I spun them yarns about the west—
    And *all* involving Me!
I represented how I'd slain
The bison on the gore-smeared plain,
    And divers tales of wonder
  I told of how I'd fought and bled
In Injun scrimmages galore,
Till Mrs. Hawthorne quoth, "No more!"
  And packed her darlings off to bed
    To dream of blood and thunder!

They must have changed a deal since then:
    The misses tall and fair,
And those three lusty, handsome men,
Would they be girls and boys again

Were I to happen there,
Down in that spot beside the sea
Where we made such tumultuous glee
In dull autumnal weather?
Ah me! the years go swiftly by,
And yet how fondly I recall
The week when we were children all—
Dear Hawthorne children, you and I—
Just eight of us, together!

LITTLE BLUE PIGEON

SLEEP, little pigeon, and fold your wings—
Little blue pigeon with velvet eyes;
Sleep to the singing of mother-bird swinging—
Swinging the nest where her little one lies.

Away out yonder I see a star—
Silvery star with a tinkling song;
To the soft dew falling I hear it calling—
Calling and tinkling the night along.

In through the window a moonbeam comes—
Little gold moonbeam with misty wings;
All silently creeping, it asks: "Is he sleeping—
Sleeping and dreaming while mother sings?"

Up from the sea there floats the sob
Of the waves that are breaking upon the shore,
As though they were groaning in anguish, and moaning—
Bemoaning the ship that shall come no more.

But sleep, little pigeon, and fold your wings—
　　Little blue pigeon with mournful eyes;
Am I not singing?—see, I am swinging—
　　Swinging the nest where my darling lies.

THE LYTTEL BOY

SOME time there ben a lyttel boy
　　That wolde not renne and play,
And helpless like that little tyke
　　Ben allwais in the way.
"Goe, make you merrie with the rest,"
　　His weary moder cried;
But with a frown he catcht her gown
　　And hong untill her side.

That boy did love his moder well,
　　Which spake him faire, I ween;
He loved to stand and hold her hand
　　And ken her with his een;
His cosset bleated in the croft,
　　His toys unheeded lay,—
He wolde not goe, but, tarrying soe,
　　Ben allwais in the way.

Godde loveth children and doth gird
　　His throne with soche as these,
And he doth smile in plaisaunce while
　　They cluster at his knees;
And some time, when he looked on earth
　　And watched the bairns at play,
He kenned with joy a lyttel boy
　　Ben allwais in the way.

And then a moder felt her heart
　　How that it ben to-torne,
She kissed eche day till she ben gray
　　The shoon he use to worn;
No bairn let hold untill her gown
　　Nor played upon the floore,—
Godde's was the joy; a lyttel boy
　　Ben in the way no more!

TEENY-WEENY

EVERY evening, after tea,
　　Teeny-Weeny comes to me,
And, astride my willing knee,
　　Plies his lash and rides away;
Though that palfrey, all too spare,
Finds his burden hard to bear,
Teeny-Weeny doesn't care;
　　He commands, and I obey!

First it's trot, and gallop then;
Now it's back to trot again;
Teeny-Weeny likes it when
　　He is riding fierce and fast.
Then his dark eyes brighter grow
And his cheeks are all aglow:
"More!" he cries, and never "Whoa!"
　　Till the horse breaks down at last.

Oh, the strange and lovely sights
Teeny-Weeny sees of nights,
As he makes those famous flights
　　On that wondrous horse of his!

Oftentimes before he knows,
Wearylike his eyelids close,
And, still smiling, off he goes
    Where the land of By-low is.

There he sees the folk of fay
Hard at ring-a-rosie play,
And he hears those fairies say:
    "Come, let's chase him to and fro!"
But, with a defiant shout,
Teeny puts that host to rout;
Of this tale I make no doubt,
    Every night he tells it so.

So I feel a tender pride
In my boy who dares to ride
That fierce horse of his astride,
    Off into those misty lands;
And as on my breast he lies,
Dreaming in that wondrous wise,
I caress his folded eyes,
    Pat his little dimpled hands.

On a time he went away,
Just a little while to stay,
And I'm not ashamed to say
    I was very lonely then;
Life without him was so sad,
You can fancy I was glad
And made merry when I had
    Teeny-Weeny back again!

So of evenings, after tea,
When he toddles up to me
And goes tugging at my knee,
    You should hear his palfrey neigh!

You should see him prance and shy,
When, with an exulting cry,
Teeny-Weeny, vaulting high,
  Plies his lash and rides away!

NELLIE

HIS listening soul hears no echo of battle,
  No pæan of triumph nor welcome of fame;
But down through the years comes a little one's prattle,
  And softly he murmurs her idolized name.
And it seems as if now at his heart she were clinging
  As she clung in those dear, distant years to his knee;
He sees her fair face, and he hears her sweet singing—
  And Nellie is coming from over the sea.

While each patriot's hope stays the fulness of sorrow,
  While our eyes are bedimmed and our voices are low,
He dreams of the daughter who comes with the morrow
  Like an angel come back from the dear long ago.
Ah, what to him now is a nation's emotion,
  And what for our love or our grief careth he?
A swift-speeding ship is a-sail on the ocean,
  And Nellie is coming from over the sea!

O daughter—my daughter! when Death stands before me
    And beckons me off to that far misty shore,
Let me see your loved form bending tenderly o'er me,
    And feel your dear kiss on my lips as of yore.
In the grace of your love all my anguish abating,
    I'll bear myself bravely and proudly as he,
And know the sweet peace that hallowed his waiting
    When Nellie was coming from over the sea.

NORSE LULLABY

THE sky is dark and the hills are white
    As the storm-king speeds from the north
      to-night;
And this is the song the storm-king sings,
As over the world his cloak he flings:
    "Sleep, sleep, little one, sleep";
He rustles his wings and gruffly sings:
    "Sleep, little one, sleep."

On yonder mountain-side a vine
Clings at the foot of a mother pine;
The tree bends over the trembling thing,
And only the vine can hear her sing:
    "Sleep, sleep, little one, sleep—
What shall you fear when I am here?
    Sleep, little one, sleep."

The king may sing in his bitter flight,
The tree may croon to the vine to-night,
But the little snowflake at my breast
Liketh the song *I* sing the best—
    Sleep, sleep, little one, sleep;
Weary thou art, a-next my heart
    Sleep, little one, sleep.

THE SUGAR-PLUM TREE

HAVE you ever heard of the Sugar-Plum Tree?
　　'Tis a marvel of great renown!
It blooms on the shore of the Lollipop sea
　　In the garden of Shut-Eye Town;
The fruit that it bears is so wondrously sweet
　　(As those who have tasted it say)
That good little children have only to eat
　　Of that fruit to be happy next day.

When you've got to the tree, you would have a hard time
　　To capture the fruit which I sing;
The tree is so tall that no person could climb
　　To the boughs where the sugar-plums swing!
But up in that tree sits a chocolate cat,
　　And a gingerbread dog prowls below—
And this is the way you contrive to get at
　　Those sugar-plums tempting you so:

You say but the word to that gingerbread dog
　　And he barks with such terrible zest
That the chocolate cat is at once all agog,
　　As her swelling proportions attest.
And the chocolate cat goes cavorting around
　　From this leafy limb unto that,
And the sugar-plums tumble, of course, to the ground—
　　Hurrah for that chocolate cat!

There are marshmallows, gumdrops, and peppermint canes,
　　With stripings of scarlet or gold,
And you carry away of the treasure that rains
　　As much as your apron can hold!
So come, little child, cuddle closer to me
　　In your dainty white nightcap and gown,
And I'll rock you away to that Sugar-Plum Tree
　　In the garden of Shut-Eye Town.

GRANDMA'S PRAYER

I PRAY that, risen from the dead,
　　I may in glory stand—
A crown, perhaps, upon my head,
　　But a needle in my hand.

I've never learned to sing or play,
　　So let no harp be mine;
From birth unto my dying day,
　　Plain sewing's been my line.

Therefore, accustomed to the end
　　To plying useful stitches,
I'll be content if asked to mend
　　The little angels' breeches.

SOME TIME

LAST night, my darling, as you slept,
　　I thought I heard you sigh,
And to your little crib I crept,
　　And watched a space thereby;
Then, bending down, I kissed your brow—
　　For, oh! I love you so—
You are too young to know it now,
　　But some time you shall know.

Some time, when, in a darkened place
　　Where others come to weep,
Your eyes shall see a weary face
　　Calm in eternal sleep;
The speechless lips, the wrinkled brow,

The patient smile may show—
You are too young to know it now,
But some time you shall know.

Look backward, then, into the years,
And see me here to-night—
See, O my darling! how my tears
Are falling as I write;
And feel once more upon your brow
The kiss of long ago—
You are too young to know it now,
But some time you shall know.

THE FIRE-HANGBIRD'S NEST

AS I am sitting in the sun upon the porch to-day,
I look with wonder at the elm that stands across the way;
I say and mean "with wonder," for now it seems to me
That elm is not as tall as years ago it used to be!
The old fire-hangbird's built her nest therein for many springs—
High up amid the sportive winds the curious cradle swings,
But not so high as when a little boy I did my best
To scale that elm and carry off the old fire-hangbird's nest!

The Hubbard boys had tried in vain to reach the homely prize
That dangled from that upper outer twig in taunting wise,
And once, when Deacon Turner's boy had almost grasped the limb,
He fell! and had to have a doctor operate on him!
Philetus Baker broke his leg and Orrin Root his arm—
But what of that? The danger gave the sport a special charm!
The Bixby and the Cutler boys, the Newtons and the rest
Ran every risk to carry off the old fire-hangbird's nest!

I can remember that I used to knee my trousers through,
That mother used to wonder how my legs got black and blue,
And how she used to talk to me and make stern threats when she
Discovered that my hobby was the nest in yonder tree;
How, as she patched my trousers or greased my purple legs,
She told me 'twould be wicked to destroy a hangbird's eggs,
And then she'd call on father and on gran'pa to attest
That they, as boys, had never robbed an old fire-hangbird's nest!

Yet all those years I coveted the trophy flaunting there,
While, as it were in mockery of my abject despair,
The old fire-hangbird confidently used to come and go,
As if she were indifferent to the bandit horde below!
And sometimes clinging to her nest we thought we heard her chide
The callow brood whose cries betrayed the fear that reigned in-
     side:
"Hush, little dears! all profitless shall be their wicked quest—
I knew my business when I built the old fire-hangbird's nest!"

For many, very many years that mother-bird has come
To rear her pretty little brood within that cosey home.
She is the selfsame bird of old—I'm certain it is she—
Although the chances are that she has quite forgotten me.
Just as of old that prudent, crafty bird of compound name
(And in parenthesis I'll say her nest is still the same);
Just as of old the passion, too, that fires the youthful breast
To climb unto and comprehend the old fire-hangbird's nest!

I like to see my old-time friend swing in that ancient tree,
And, if the elm's as tall and sturdy as it *used* to be,
I'm sure that many a year that nest shall in the breezes blow,
For boys aren't what they used to be a forty years ago!
The elm looks shorter than it did when Brother Rufe and I
Beheld with envious hearts that trophy flaunted from on high;
He writes that in the city where he's living 'way out West
His little boys have never seen an old fire-hangbird's nest!

Poor little chaps! how lonesomelike their city life must be—
I wish they'd come and live awhile in this old house with me!
They'd have the honest friends and healthful sports I used to know
When Brother Rufe and I were boys a forty years ago.
So, when they grew from romping lads to busy, useful men,
They could recall with proper pride their country life again;
And of those recollections of their youth I'm sure the best
Would be of how they sought in vain the old fire-hangbird's nest!

BUTTERCUP, POPPY, FORGET-ME-NOT

BUTTERCUP, Poppy, Forget-me-not—
These three bloomed in a garden spot;
And once, all merry with song and play,
A little one heard three voices say:
"Shine and shadow, summer and spring,
O thou child with the tangled hair

22

And laughing eyes! we three shall bring
 Each an offering passing fair."
The little one did not understand,
But they bent and kissed the dimpled hand.

Buttercup gambolled all day long,
Sharing the little one's mirth and song;
Then, stealing along on misty gleams,
Poppy came bearing the sweetest dreams.
 Playing and dreaming—and that was all,
  Till once a sleeper would not awake;
 Kissing the little face under the pall,
  We thought of the words the third flower spake;
And we found betimes in a hallowed spot
The solace and peace of Forget-me-not.

Buttercup shareth the joy of day,
Glinting with gold the hours of play;
Bringeth the Poppy sweet repose,
When the hands would fold and the eyes would close;
 And after it all—the play and the sleep
  Of a little life—what cometh then?
 To the hearts that ache and the eyes that weep
  A new flower bringeth God's peace again.
Each one serveth its tender lot—
Buttercup, Poppy, Forget-me-not.

GOLD AND LOVE FOR DEARIE

OUT on the mountain over the town,
 All night long, all night long,
The trolls go up and the trolls go down,

Bearing their packs and singing a song;
And this is the song the hill-folk croon,
As they trudge in the light of the misty moon—
This is ever their dolorous tune:
"Gold, gold! ever more gold—
	Bright red gold for dearie!"

Deep in the hill a father delves
	All night long, all night long;
None but the peering, furtive elves
	Sees his toil and hears his song;
Merrily ever the cavern rings
As merrily ever his pick he swings,
And merrily ever this song he sings:
"Gold, gold! ever more gold—
	Bright red gold for dearie!"

Mother is rocking thy lowly bed
	All night long, all night long,
Happy to smooth thy curly head,
	To hold thy hand and to sing *her* song:
'Tis not of the hill-folk dwarfed and old,
Nor the song of thy father, stanch and bold,
And the burthen it beareth is not of gold;
But it's "Love, love! nothing but love—
	Mother's love for dearie!"

THE PEACE OF CHRISTMAS-TIME

DEAREST, how hard it is to say
	That all is for the best,'
Since, sometimes, in a grievous way
	God's will is manifest.

See with what hearty, noisy glee
   Our little ones to-night
Dance round and round our Christmas tree
   With pretty toys bedight.

Dearest, one voice they may not hear,
   One face they may not see—
Ah, what of all this Christmas cheer
   Cometh to you and me?

Cometh before our misty eyes
   That other little face,
And we clasp, in tender, reverent wise,
   That love in the old embrace.

Dearest, the Christ-Child walks to-night,
   Bringing his peace to men,
And he bringeth to you and to me the light
   Of the old, old years again.

Bringeth the peace of long ago,
   When a wee one clasped your knee
And lisped of the morrow—dear one, you know—
   And here come back is he!

Dearest, 'tis sometimes hard to say
   That all is for the best,
For, often, in a grievous way
   God's will is manifest.

But in the grace of this holy night
   That bringeth us back our child,
Let us see that the ways of God are right,
   And so be reconciled.

TO A LITTLE BROOK

YOU'RE not so big as you were then,
   O little brook!—
I mean those hazy summers when
We boys roamed, full of awe, beside
Your noisy, foaming, tumbling tide,
And wondered if it could be true
That there were bigger brooks than you,
   O mighty brook, O peerless brook!

All up and down this reedy place
   Where lives the brook,
We angled for the furtive dace;
The redwing-blackbird did his best
To make us think he'd build his nest
Hard by the stream, when, like as not,
He'd hung it in a secret spot
   Far from the brook, the telltale brook!

And often, when the noontime heat
   Parboiled the brook,
We'd draw our boots and swing our feet
Upon the waves that, in their play,
Would tag us last and scoot away;
And mother never seemed to know
What burnt our legs and chapped them so—
   But father guessed it was the brook!

And Fido—how he loved to swim
   The cooling brook,
Whenever we'd throw sticks for him;
And how we boys *did* wish that we
Could only swim as good as he—
Why, Daniel Webster never was
Recipient of such great applause
   As Fido, battling with the brook!

But once—O most unhappy day
   For you, my brook!—
Came Cousin Sam along that way;
And, having lived a spell out West,
Where creeks aren't counted much at best,
He neither waded, swam, nor leapt,
But, with superb indifference, *stept*
   Across that brook—our mighty brook!

Why do you scamper on your way,
   You little brook,
When I come back to you to-day?
Is it because you flee the grass
That lunges at you as you pass,
As if, in playful mood, it would
Tickle the truant if it could,
   You chuckling brook—you saucy brook?

Or is it you no longer know—
   You fickle brook—
The honest friend of long ago?
The years that kept us twain apart
Have changed my face, but not my heart—
Many and sore those years, and yet
I fancied you could not forget
   That happy time, my playmate brook!

Oh, sing again in artless glee,
   My little brook,
The song you used to sing for me—
The song that's lingered in my ears
So soothingly these many years;
My grief shall be forgotten when
I hear your tranquil voice again
   And that sweet song, dear little brook!

CROODLIN' DOO

HO, pretty bee, did you see my croodlin' doo?
　　　Ho, little lamb, is she jinkin' on the lea?
　　　Ho, bonnie fairy, bring my dearie back to me—
Got a lump o' sugar an' a posie for you,
Only bring me back my wee, wee croodlin' doo!

Why! here you are, my little croodlin' doo!
　　　Looked in er cradle, but didn't find you there—
　　　Looked f'r my wee, wee croodlin' doo ever'where;
Be'en kind lonesome all er day withouten you—
Where you be'n, my teeny, wee, wee croodlin' doo?

Now you go balow, my little croodlin' doo;
　　　Now you go rockaby ever so far,—
　　　Rockaby, rockaby up to the star
That's winkin' an' blinkin' an' singin' to you,
As you go balow, my wee, wee croodlin' doo!

LITTLE MISTRESS SANS-MERCI

LITTLE Mistress Sans-Merci
　　Fareth world-wide, fancy free:
　　Trotteth cooing to and fro,
　　　And her cooing is command—
　　Never ruled there yet, I trow,
　　　Mightier despot in the land.
And my heart it lieth where
Mistress Sans-Merci doth fare.

Little Mistress Sans-Merci—
She hath made a slave of me!
　　"Go," she biddeth, and I go—
　　　"Come," and I am fain to come—

Never mercy doth she show,
  Be she wroth or frolicsome,
Yet am I content to be
Slave to Mistress Sans-Merci!

Little Mistress Sans-Merci
Hath become so dear to me
  That I count as passing sweet
    All the pain her moods impart,
  And I bless the little feet
    That go trampling on my heart:
Ah, how lonely life would be
But for little Sans-Merci!

Little Mistress Sans-Merci,
Cuddle close this night to me,
  And the heart, which all day long
    Ruthless thou hast trod upon,
  Shall outpour a soothing song
    For its best-belovèd one—
All its tenderness for thee,
Little Mistress Sans-Merci!

LONG AGO

I ONCE knew all the birds that came
  And nested in our orchard trees,
For every flower I had a name,—
  My friends were woodchucks, toads, and bees;
I knew where thrived in yonder glen
  What plants would soothe a stone-bruised toe—
Oh, I was very learned then,
  But that was very long ago.

I knew the spot upon the hill
  Where checkerberries could be found,
I knew the rushes near the mill
  Where pickerel lay that weighed a pound!
I knew the wood—the very tree
  Where lived the poaching, saucy crow,
And all the woods and crows knew me—
  But that was very long ago.

And pining for the joys of youth,
  I tread the old familiar spot
Only to learn this solemn truth:
  I have forgotten, am forgot.
Yet here's this youngster at my knee
  Knows all the things I used to know;
To think I once was wise as he!—
  But that was very long ago.

I know it's folly to complain
  Of whatsoe'er the fates decree,
Yet, were not wishes all in vain,
  I tell you what my wish should be:
I'd wish to be a boy again,
  Back with the friends I used to know.
For I was, oh, so happy then—
  But that was very long ago!

IN THE FIRELIGHT

THE fire upon the hearth is low,
    And there is stillness everywhere,
      And, like wing'd spirits, here and there
The firelight shadows fluttering go.
And as the shadows round me creep,

A childish treble breaks the gloom,
And softly from a further room
Comes: "Now I lay me down to sleep."

And, somehow, with that little pray'r
And that sweet treble in my ears,
My thought goes back to distant years,
And lingers with a dear one there;
And as I hear my child's amen,
My mother's faith comes back to me—
Crouched at her side I seem to be,
And mother holds my hands again.

Oh, for an hour in that dear place—
Oh, for the peace of that dear time—
Oh, for that childish trust sublime—
Oh, for a glimpse of mother's face!
Yet, as the shadows round me creep,
I do not seem to be alone—
Sweet magic of that treble tone
And "Now I lay me down to sleep!"

COBBLER AND STORK

Cobbler.

STORK, I am justly wroth,
For thou hast wronged me sore;
The ash roof-tree that shelters thee
Shall shelter thee no more!

Stork.

Full fifty years I've dwelt
　　Upon this honest tree,
And long ago (as people know!)
　　I brought thy father thee.
What hail hath chilled thy heart,
　　That thou shouldst bid me go?
Speak out, I pray—then I'll away,
　　Since thou commandest so.

Cobbler.

Thou tellest of the time
　　When, wheeling from the west,
This hut thou sought'st and one
　　　　thou brought'st
Unto a mother's breast.
I was the wretched child
　　Was fetched that dismal morn—
'Twere better die than be (as I)
　　To life of misery born!
And hadst thou borne me on
　　Still farther up the town,
A king I'd be of high degree,
　　And wear a golden crown!
For yonder lives the prince
　　Was brought that selfsame day:
How happy he, while—look at me!
　　I toil my life away!
And see my little boy—
　　To what estate he's born!
Why, when I die no hoard leave I
　　But poverty and scorn.
And *thou* hast done it all—
　　I might have been a king
And ruled in state, but for thy hate,
　　Thou base, perfidious thing!

Stork.

Since, cobbler, thou dost speak
    Of one thou lovest well,
Hear of that king what grievous thing
    This very morn befell.
Whilst round thy homely bench
    Thy well-belovèd played,
In yonder hall beneath a pall
    A little one was laid;
Thy well-belovèd's face
    Was rosy with delight,
But 'neath that pall in yonder hall
    The little face is white;
Whilst by a merry voice
    Thy soul is filled with cheer,
Another weeps for one that sleeps
    All mute and cold anear;
One father hath his hope,
    And one is childless now;
He wears a crown and rules a town—
    Only a cobbler *thou!*
Wouldst thou exchange thy lot
    At price of such a woe?
I'll nest no more above thy door,
    But, as thou bidst me, go.

Cobbler.

Nay, stork! thou shalt remain—
    I mean not what I said;
Good neighbors we must always be,
    So make thy home o'erhead.
I would not change my bench
    For any monarch's throne,
Nor sacrifice at any price
    My darling and my own!

Stork! on my roof-tree bide,
That, seeing thee anear,
I'll thankful be God sent by thee
Me and my darling here!

"LOLLYBY, LOLLY, LOLLYBY"

LAST night, whiles that the curfew bell ben ringing,
I heard a moder to her dearie singing,
    "Lollyby, lolly, lollyby";
And presently that chylde did cease hys weeping,
And on his moder's breast did fall a-sleeping
    To "lolly, lolly, lollyby."

Faire ben the chylde unto his moder clinging,
But fairer yet the moder's gentle singing—
    "Lollyby, lolly, lollyby";
And angels came and kisst the dearie smiling
In dreems while him hys moder ben beguiling
    With "lolly, lolly, lollyby."

Then to my harte saies I: "Oh, that thy beating
Colde be assuaged by some sweete voice repeating
    'Lollyby, lolly, lollyby';

That like this lyttel chylde I, too, ben sleeping
With plaisaunt phantasies about me creeping,
To 'lolly, lolly, lollyby'!"

Some time—mayhap when curfew bells are ringing—
A weary harte shall heare straunge voices singing
"Lollyby, lolly, lollyby";
Some time, mayhap, with Chryst's love round me
streaming,
I shall be lulled into eternal dreeming,
With "lolly, lolly, lollyby."

LIZZIE AND THE BABY

I WONDER ef all wimmin air
Like Lizzie is when we go out
To theatres an' concerts where
Is things the papers talk about.
Do other wimmin fret an' stew
Like they wuz bein' crucified—
Frettin' a show or concert through,
With wonderin' ef the baby cried?

Now Lizzie knows that gran'ma's there
To see that everything is right,
Yet Lizzie thinks that gran'ma's care
Ain't good enuff f'r baby, quite;
Yet what am I to answer when
She kind uv fidgets at my side,
An' asks me every now and then:
"I wonder if the baby cried?"

Seems like she seen two little eyes
  A-pinin' f'r their mother's smile—
Seems like she heern the pleadin' cries
  Uv one she thinks uv all the while;
An' so she's sorry that she come,
  An' though she allus tries to hide
The truth, she'd ruther stay to hum
  Than wonder ef the baby cried.

Yes, wimmin folks is all alike—
  By Lizzie you kin jedge the rest;
There never wuz a little tyke,
  But that his mother loved him best.
And nex' to bein' what I be—
  The husband uv my gentle bride—
I'd wisht I wuz that croodlin' wee
  With Lizzie wonderin' ef I cried.

AT THE DOOR

I THOUGHT myself, indeed, secure
  So fast the door, so firm the lock;
But, lo! he toddling comes to lure
  My parent ear with timorous knock.

My heart were stone could it withstand
  The sweetness of my baby's plea,—
That timorous, baby knocking and
  "Please let me in,—it's only me."

I threw aside the unfinished book,
  Regardless of its tempting charms,
And, opening wide the door, I took
  My laughing darling in my arms.

Who knows but in Eternity,
   I, like a truant child, shall wait
The glories of a life to be,
   Beyond the Heavenly Father's gate?

And will that Heavenly Father heed
   The truant's supplicating cry,
As at the outer door I plead,
   " 'Tis I, O Father! only I"?

HUGO'S "CHILD AT PLAY"

A CHILD was singing at his play—
   I heard the song, and paused to hear;
His mother moaning, groaning lay,
   And, lo! a spectre stood anear!

The child shook sunlight from his hair,
   And carolled gayly all day long—
Aye, with that spectre gloating there,
   The innocent made mirth and song!

How like to harvest fruit wert thou,
   O sorrow, in that dismal room—
God ladeth not the tender bough
   Save with the joy of bud and bloom!

WYNKEN, BLYNKEN, AND NOD

WYNKEN, Blynken, and Nod one night
    Sailed off in a wooden shoe—
Sailed on a river of crystal light,
    Into a sea of dew.
"Where are you going, and what do you wish?"
    The old moon asked the three.
"We have come to fish for the herring fish
    That live in this beautiful sea;
    Nets of silver and gold have we!"
           Said Wynken,
           Blynken,
           And Nod.

The old moon laughed and sang a song,
    As they rocked in the wooden shoe,
And the wind that sped them all night long
    Ruffled the waves of dew.
The little stars were the herring fish
    That lived in that beautiful sea—
"Now cast your nets wherever you wish—
    Never afeard are we";
    So cried the stars to the fishermen three:
           Wynken,
           Blynken,
           And Nod.

All night long their nets they threw
    To the stars in the twinkling foam—
Then down from the skies came the wooden shoe,
    Bringing the fishermen home;
'Twas all so pretty a sail it seemed
    As if it could not be,
And some folks thought 'twas a dream they'd dreamed
    Of sailing that beautiful sea—

But I shall name you the fishermen three:
        Wynken,
        Blynken,
        And Nod.

Wynken and Blynken are two little eyes,
   And Nod is a little head,
And the wooden shoe that sailed the skies
   Is a wee one's trundle-bed.
So shut your eyes while mother sings
   Of wonderful sights that be,
And you shall see the beautiful things
   As you rock in the misty sea,
   Where the old shoe rocked the fishermen three:
        Wynken,
        Blynken,
        And Nod.

LITTLE BOY BLUE

THE little toy dog is covered with dust,
   But sturdy and staunch he stands;
And the little toy soldier is red with rust,
   And his musket moulds in his hands.
Time was when the little toy dog was new,
   And the soldier was passing fair;
And that was the time when our Little Boy Blue
   Kissed them and put them there.

"Now, don't you go till I come," he said,
   "And don't you make any noise!"
So, toddling off to his trundle-bed,
   He dreamt of the pretty toys;

And, as he was dreaming, an angel song
    Awakened our Little Boy Blue—
Oh! the years are many, the years are long,
    But the little toy friends are true!

Aye, faithful to Little Boy Blue they stand,
    Each in the same old place—
Awaiting the touch of a little hand,
    The smile of a little face;
And they wonder, as waiting the long years through
    In the dust of that little chair,
What has become of our Little Boy Blue,
    Since he kissed them and put them there.

FATHER'S LETTER

I'M going to write a letter to our oldest boy who went
    Out West last spring to practise law and run for president;
I'll tell him all the gossip I guess he'd like to hear,
For he hasn't seen the home-folks for going on a year!
Most generally it's Marthy does the writing, but as she
Is suffering with a felon, why, the job devolves on me—
So, when the supper things are done and put away to-night,
I'll draw my boots and shed my coat and settle down to write.

I'll tell him crops are looking up, with prospects big for corn,
That, fooling with the barnyard gate, the off-ox hurt his horn;
That the Templar lodge is doing well—Tim Bennett joined last
        week
When the prohibition candidate for Congress came to speak;
That the old gray woodchuck's living still down in the pasture-lot,
A-wondering what's become of little William, like as not!
Oh, yes, there's lots of pleasant things and no bad news to tell,
Except that old Bill Graves was sick, but now he's up and well.

Cy Cooper says—(but I'll not pass my word that it is so,
For Cy he is some punkins on spinning yarns, you know)—
He says that, since the freshet, the pickerel are so thick
In Baker's pond you can wade in and kill 'em with a stick!
The Hubbard girls are teaching school, and Widow Cutler's Bill
Has taken Eli Baxter's place in Luther Eastman's mill;
Old Deacon Skinner's dog licked Deacon Howard's dog last week,
And now there are two lambkins in one flock that will not speak.

The yellow rooster froze his feet, a-wadin' through the snow,
And now he leans agin the fence when he starts in to crow;
The chestnut colt that was so skittish when *he* went away—
I've broke him to the sulky and I drive him every day!
We've got pink window curtains for the front spare-room up-stairs,
And Lizzie's made new covers for the parlor lounge and chairs;
We've roofed the barn and braced the elm that has the hang-bird's
        nest—
Oh, there's been lots of changes since our William went out West!

Old Uncle Enos Packard is getting mighty gay—
He gave Miss Susan Birchard a peach the other day!
His late lamented Sarah hain't been buried quite a year,
So his purring 'round Miss Susan causes criticism here.
At the last donation party, the minister opined
That, if he'd half suspicioned what was coming, he'd resigned;
For, though they brought him slippers like he was a centipede,
His pantry was depleted by the consequential feed!

These are the things I'll write him—our boy that's in the West;
And I'll tell him how we miss him—his mother and the rest;
Why, we never have an apple-pie that mother doesn't say:
"*He* liked it so—I wish that he could have a piece to-day!"
I'll tell him we are prospering, and hope he is the same—
That we hope he'll have no trouble getting on to wealth and fame;
And just before I write "good-by from father and the rest,"
I'll say that "mother sends her love," and that will please him best.

For when *I* went away from home, the weekly news I heard
Was nothing to the tenderness I found in that one word—
The sacred name of mother—why, even now as then,
The thought brings back the saintly face, the gracious love again;
And in my bosom seems to come a peace that is divine,
As if an angel spirit communed a while with mine;
And one man's heart is strengthened by the message from above,
And earth seems nearer heaven when "mother sends her love."

JEWISH LULLABY

MY harp is on the willow-tree,
Else would I sing, O love, to thee
A song of long-ago—
Perchance the song that Miriam sung
Ere yet Judea's heart was wrung
By centuries of woe.

I ate my crust in tears to-day,
As scourged I went upon my way—
And yet my darling smiled;
Aye, beating at my breast, he laughed—
My anguish curdled not the draught—
'Twas sweet with love, my child!

The shadow of the centuries lies
Deep in thy dark and mournful eyes;
But, hush! and close them now,
And in the dreams that thou shalt dream
The light of other days shall seem
To glorify thy brow!

Our harp is on the willow-tree—
I have no song to sing to thee,
    As shadows round us roll;
But, hush and sleep, and thou shalt hear
Jehovah's voice that speaks to cheer
    Judea's fainting soul!

OUR WHIPPINGS

COME, Harvey, let us sit a while and talk about the times
    Before you went to selling clothes and I to peddling rimes—
The days when we were little boys, as naughty little boys
As ever worried home-folks with their everlasting noise!
Egad! and, were we so disposed, I'll venture we could show
The scars of wallopings we got some forty years ago;
What wallopings I mean I think I need not specify—
Mother's whippings didn't hurt, but father's! oh, my!

The way that we played hookey those many years ago—
We'd rather give 'most anything than have our children know!
The thousand naughty things we did, the thousand fibs we told—
Why, thinking of them makes my Presbyterian blood run cold!
How often Deacon Sabine Morse remarked if we were his
He'd tan our "pesky little hides until the blisters riz"!
It's many a hearty thrashing to that Deacon Morse we owe—
Mother's whippings didn't count—father's did, though!

We used to sneak off swimmin' in those careless, boyish days,
And come back home of evenings with our necks and backs ablaze;
How mother used to wonder why our clothes were full of sand,
But father, having been a boy, appeared to understand.
And, after tea, he'd beckon us to join him in the shed
Where he'd proceed to tinge our backs a deeper, darker red;
Say what we will of mother's, there is none will controvert
The proposition that our father's lickings always hurt!

For mother was by nature so forgiving and so mild
That she inclined to spare the rod although she spoiled the child;
And when at last in self-defence she had to whip us, she
Appeared to feel those whippings a great deal more than we!
But how we bellowed and took on, as if we'd like to die—
Poor mother really thought she hurt, and that's what made *her* cry!
Then how we youngsters snickered as out the door we slid,
For mother's whippings never hurt, though father's always did.

In after years poor father simmered down to five feet four,
But in our youth he seemed to us in height eight feet or more!
Oh, how we shivered when he quoth in cold, suggestive tone:
"I'll see you in the woodshed after supper all alone!"

Oh, how the legs and arms and dust and trouser buttons flew—
What florid vocalisms marked that vesper interview!
Yes, after all this lapse of years, I feelingly assert,
With all respect to mother, it was father's whippings hurt!

The little boy experiencing that tingling 'neath his vest
Is often loath to realize that all is for the best;
Yet, when the boy gets older, he pictures with delight
The buffetings of childhood—as we do here to-night.
The years, the gracious years, have smoothed and beautified the
        ways
That to our little feet seemed all too rugged in the days
Before you went to selling clothes and I to peddling rimes—
So, Harvey, let us sit a while and think upon those times.

THE ARMENIAN MOTHER

I WAS a mother, and I weep;
        The night is come—the day is sped—
The night of woe profound, for, oh,
        My little golden son is dead!

The pretty rose that bloomed anon
        Upon my mother breast, they stole;
They let the dove I nursed with love
        Fly far away—so sped my soul!

That falcon Death swooped down upon
        My sweet-voiced turtle as he sung;
'Tis hushed and dark where soared the lark
        And so, and so my heart was wrung!

Before my eyes, they sent the hail
 Upon my green pomegranate-tree—
Upon the bough where only now
 A rosy apple bent to me.

They shook my beauteous almond-tree,
 Beating its glorious bloom to death—
They strewed it round upon the ground,
 And mocked its fragrant dying breath.

I was a mother, and I weep;
 I seek the rose where nestleth none—
No more is heard the singing bird—
 I have no little golden son!

So fall the shadows over me,
 The blighted garden, lonely nest.
Reach down in love, O God above!
 And fold my darling to thy breast.

HEIGHO, MY DEARIE

A MOONBEAM floateth from the skies,
     Whispering: "Heigho, my dearie;
I would spin a web before your eyes—
A beautiful web of silver light
Wherein is many a wondrous sight
Of a radiant garden leagues away,
Where the softly tinkling lilies sway
And the snow-white lambkins are at play—
     Heigho, my dearie!"

A brownie stealeth from the vine,
     Singing: "Heigho, my dearie;
And will you hear this song of mine—
A song of the land of murk and mist
Where bideth the bud the dew hath kist?
Then let the moonbeam's web of light
Be spun before thee silvery white,
And I shall sing the livelong night—
     Heigho, my dearie!"

The night wind speedeth from the sea,
     Murmuring: "Heigho, my dearie;
I bring a mariner's prayer for thee;
So let the moonbeam veil thine eyes,
And the brownie sing thee lullabies—
But I shall rock thee to and fro,
Kissing the brow *he* loveth so.
And the prayer shall guard thy bed, I trow—
     Heigho, my dearie!"

TO A USURPER

AHA! a traitor in the camp,
    A rebel strangely bold,—
A lisping, laughing, toddling scamp,
    Not more than four years old!

To think that I, who've ruled alone
    So proudly in the past,
Should be ejected from my throne
    By my own son at last!

He trots his treason to and fro,
    As only babies can,
And says he'll be his mamma's beau
    When he's a "gweat, big man"!

You stingy boy! you've always had
    A share in mamma's heart.
Would you begrudge your poor old dad
    The tiniest little part?

That mamma, I regret to see,
    Inclines to take your part,—
As if a dual monarchy
    Should rule her gentle heart!

But when the years of youth have sped,
    The bearded man, I trow,
Will quite forget he ever said
    He'd be his mamma's beau.

Renounce your treason, little son,
    Leave mamma's heart to me;
For there will come another one
    To claim your loyalty.

And when that other comes to you,
　God grant her love may shine
Through all your life, as fair and true
　As mamma's does through mine!

THE BELL-FLOWER TREE

WHEN Brother Bill and I were boys,
　　How often in the summer we
Would seek the shade your branches made,
　O fair and gracious bell-flower tree!
Amid the clover bloom we sat
　And looked upon the Holyoke range,
While Fido lay a space away,
　Thinking our silence very strange.

The woodchuck in the pasture-lot,
　Beside his furtive hole elate,
Heard, off beyond the pickerel pond,
　The redwing-blackbird chide her mate.
The bumblebee went bustling round,
　Pursuing labors never done—
With drone and sting, the greedy thing
　Begrudged the sweets we lay upon!

Our eyes looked always at the hills—
　The Holyoke hills that seemed to stand
Between us boys and pictured joys
　Of conquest in a further land!
Ah, how we coveted the time
　When we should leave this prosy place
And work our wills beyond those hills,
　And meet creation face to face!

You must have heard our childish talk—
    Perhaps our prattle gave you pain;
For then, old friend, you seemed to bend
    Your kindly arms about us twain.
It might have been the wind that sighed,
    And yet I thought I heard you say:
"Seek not the ills beyond those hills—
    Oh, stay with me, my children, stay!"

See, I've come back; the boy you knew
    Is wiser, older, sadder grown;
I come once more, just as of yore—
    I come, but see! I come alone!
The memory of a brother's love,
    Of blighted hopes, I bring with me,
And here I lay my heart to-day—
    A weary heart, O bell-flower tree!

So let me nestle in your shade
    As though I were a boy again,
And pray extend your arms, old friend,
    And love me as you used to then.
Sing softly as you used to sing,
    And maybe I shall seem to be
A little boy and feel the joy
    Of thy repose, O bell-flower tree!

FAIRY AND CHILD

OH, listen, little Dear-My-Soul,
  To the fairy voices calling,
For the moon is high in the misty sky
  And the honey dew is falling;
To the midnight feast in the clover bloom
  The bluebells are a-ringing,
And it's "Come away to the land of fay"
  That the katydid is singing.

Oh, slumber, little Dear-My-Soul,
  And hand in hand we'll wander—
Hand in hand to the beautiful land
  Of Balow, away off yonder;
Or we'll sail along in a lily leaf
  Into the white moon's halo—
Over a stream of mist and dream
  Into the land of Balow.

Or, you shall have two beautiful wings—
  Two gossamer wings and airy,
And all the while shall the old moon smile
  And think you a little fairy;
And you shall dance in the velvet sky,
  And the silvery stars shall twinkle
And dream sweet dreams as over their beams
  Your footfalls softly tinkle.

THE GRANDSIRE

I LOVED him so; his voice had grown
  Into my heart, and now to hear
The pretty song he had sung so long
  Die on the lips to me so dear!

He a child with golden curls,
  And I with head as white as snow—
I knelt down there and made this pray'r:
  "God, let me be the first to go!"

How often I recall it now:
  My darling tossing on his bed,
I sitting there in mute despair,
  Smoothing the curls that crowned his head.
They did not speak to me of death—
  A feeling *here* had told me so;
What could I say or do but pray
  That I might be the first to go?

Yet, thinking of him standing there
  Out yonder as the years go by,
Waiting for me to come, I see
  'Twas better he should wait, not I.
For when I walk the vale of death,
  Above the wail of Jordan's flow
Shall rise a song that shall make me strong—
  The call of the child that was first to go.

HUSHABY, SWEET MY OWN

FAIR is the castle up on the hill—
      Hushaby, sweet my own!
The night is fair, and the waves are still.
And the wind is singing to you and to me
In this lowly home beside the sea—
      Hushaby, sweet my own!

On yonder hill is store of wealth—
    Hushaby, sweet my own!
And revellers drink to a little one's health;
But you and I bide night and day
For the other love that has sailed away—
    Hushaby, sweet my own!

See not, dear eyes, the forms that creep
    Ghostlike, O my own!
Out of the mists of the murmuring deep;
Oh, see them not and make no cry
Till the angels of death have passed us by—
    Hushaby, sweet my own!

Ah, little they reck of you and me—
    Hushaby, sweet my own!
In our lonely home beside the sea;
They seek the castle up on the hill,
And there they will do their ghostly will—
    Hushaby, O my own!

Here by the sea a mother croons
    "Hushaby, sweet my own!"
In yonder castle a mother swoons
While the angels go down to the misty deep
Bearing a little one fast asleep—
    Hushaby, sweet my own!

CHILD AND MOTHER

O MOTHER-MY-LOVE, if you'll give me your hand,
    And go where I ask you to wander,
I will lead you away to a beautiful land—
    The Dreamland that's waiting out yonder.
We'll walk in a sweet-posie garden out there

Where moonlight and starlight are streaming
And the flowers and the birds are filling the air
  With the fragrance and music of dreaming.

There'll be no little tired-out boy to undress,
  No questions or cares to perplex you;
There'll be no little bruises or bumps to caress,
  Nor patching of stockings to vex you.
For I'll rock you away on a silver-dew stream,
  And sing you asleep when you're weary,
And no one shall know of our beautiful dream
  But you and your own little dearie.

And when I am tired I'll nestle my head
  In the bosom that's soothed me so often,
And the wide-awake stars shall sing in my stead
  A song which our dreaming shall soften.
So, Mother-My-Love, let me take your dear hand,
  And away through the starlight we'll wander—
Away through the mist to the beautiful land—
  The Dreamland that's waiting out yonder!

MEDIEVAL EVENTIDE SONG

COME hither, lyttel childe, and lie upon my breast tonight,
    For yonder fares an angell yclad in raimaunt white,
And yonder sings ye angell as onely angells may,
And his songe ben of a garden that bloometh farre awaye.

To them that have no lyttel childe Godde sometimes sendeth down
A lyttel childe that ben a lyttel angell of his owne;
And if so bee they love that childe, he willeth it to staye,
But elsewise, in his mercie, he taketh it awaye.

And sometimes, though they love it, Godde yearneth for ye childe,
And sendeth angells singing, whereby it ben beguiled;
They fold their arms about ye lamb that croodleth at his play,
And beare him to ye garden that bloometh farre awaye.

I wolde not lose ye lyttel lamb that Godde hath lent to me;
If I colde sing that angell songe, how joysome I sholde be!
For, with mine arms about him, and my musick in his eare,
What angell songe of paradize soever sholde I feare?

Soe come, my lyttel childe, and lie upon my breast to-night,
For yonder fares an angell yclad in raimaunt white,
And yonder sings that angell, as onely angells may,
And his songe ben of a garden that bloometh farre awaye.

THE LITTLE PEACH

A LITTLE peach in the orchard grew,—
A little peach of emerald hue;
Warmed by the sun and wet by the dew,
     It grew.

One day, passing that orchard through,
That little peach dawned on the view
Of Johnny Jones and his Sister Sue—
     Them two.

Up at that peach a club they threw—
Down from the stem on which it grew
Fell that peach of emerald hue.
        Mon Dieu!

John took a bite and Sue a chew,
And then the trouble began to brew,—
Trouble the doctor couldn't subdue.
        Too true!

Under the turf where the daisies grew
They planted John and his Sister Sue,
And their little souls to the angels flew,—
        Boo hoo!

What of that peach of the emerald hue,
Warmed by the sun, and wet by the dew?
Ah, well, its mission on earth is through.
        Adieu!

ARMENIAN LULLABY

IF thou wilt shut thy drowsy eyes,
  My mulberry one, my golden sun!
The rose shall sing thee lullabies,
  My pretty cosset lambkin!
And thou shalt swing in an almond-tree,
With a flood of moonbeams rocking thee—
A silver boat in a golden sea,
  My velvet love, my nestling dove,
    My own pomegranate blossom!

The stork shall guard thee passing well
　　All night, my sweet! my dimple-feet!
And bring thee myrrh and asphodel,
　　My gentle rain-of-springtime!
And for thy slumbrous play shall twine
The diamond stars with an emerald vine
To trail in the waves of ruby wine,
　　My myrtle bloom, my heart's perfume,
　　　My little chirping sparrow!

And when the morn wakes up to see
　　My apple bright, my soul's delight!
The partridge shall come calling thee,
　　My jar of milk-and-honey!
Yes, thou shalt know what mystery lies
In the amethyst deep of the curtained skies,
If thou wilt fold thy onyx eyes,
　　You wakeful one, you naughty son,
　　　You cooing little turtle!

CHRISTMAS TREASURES

I COUNT my treasures o'er with care,—
　　The little toy my darling knew,
　　A little sock of faded hue,
A little lock of golden hair.

Long years ago this holy time,
　　My little one—my all to me—
　　Sat robed in white upon my knee,
And heard the merry Christmas chime.

"Tell me, my little golden-head,
    If Santa Claus should come to-night,
    What shall he bring my baby bright,—
What treasure for my boy?" I said.

And then he named this little toy,
    While in his round and mournful eyes
    There came a look of sweet surprise,
That spake his quiet, trustful joy.

And as he lisped his evening prayer
    He asked the boon with childish grace;
    Then, toddling to the chimney-place,
He hung this little stocking there.

That night, while lengthening shadows crept,
    I saw the white-winged angels come
    With singing to our lowly home
And kiss my darling as he slept.

They must have heard his little prayer,
    For in the morn, with rapturous face,
    He toddled to the chimney-place,
And found this little treasure there.

They came again one Christmas-tide,—
    That angel host, so fair and white;
    And, singing all that glorious night,
They lured my darling from my side.

A little sock, a little toy,
    A little lock of golden hair,
    The Christmas music on the air,
A watching for my baby boy!

But if again that angel train
  And golden-head come back for me,
    To bear me to Eternity,
My watching will not be in vain.

OH, LITTLE CHILD

HUSH, little one, and fold your hands—
  The sun hath set, the moon is high;
The sea is singing to the sands,
    And wakeful posies are beguiled
  By many a fairy lullaby—
    Hush, little child—my little child!

Dream, little one, and in your dreams
  Float upward from this lowly place—
Float out on mellow, misty streams
    To lands where bideth Mary mild,
  And let her kiss thy little face,
    You little child—my little child!

Sleep, little one, and take thy rest—
  With angels bending over thee,
Sleep sweetly on that Father's breast
    Whom our dear Christ hath reconciled—
  But stay not there—come back to me,
    Oh, little child—*my* little child!

GANDERFEATHER'S GIFT

I WAS just a little thing
　　When a fairy came and kissed me;
Floating in upon the light
Of a haunted summer night,
Lo, the fairies came to sing
Pretty slumber songs and bring
　　Certain boons that else had missed me.
From a dream I turned to see
What those strangers brought for me,
　　When that fairy up and kissed me—
　　Here, upon this cheek, he kissed me!

Simmerdew was there, but she
　　Did not like me altogether;
Daisybright and Turtledove,
Pilfercurds and Honeylove,
Thistleblow and Amberglee
On that gleaming, ghostly sea
　　Floated from the misty heather,
And around my trundle-bed
Frisked, and looked, and whispering said—
　　Solemnlike and all together:
　　"*You* shall kiss him, Ganderfeather!"

Ganderfeather kissed me then—
　　Ganderfeather, quaint and merry!
No attenuate sprite was he,
—But as buxom as could be;—
Kissed me twice, and once again,
And the others shouted when
　　On my cheek uprose a berry
Somewhat like a mole, mayhap,
But the kiss-mark of that chap
　　Ganderfeather, passing merry—
　　Humorsome, but kindly, very!

I was just a tiny thing
    When the prankish Ganderfeather
Brought this curious gift to me
With his fairy kisses three;
Yet with honest pride I sing
That same gift he chose to bring
    Out of yonder haunted heather.
Other charms and friendships fly—
Constant friends this mole and I,
    Who have been so long together.
    Thank you, little Ganderfeather!

BAMBINO

BAMBINO in his cradle slept;
    And by his side his grandam grim
Bent down and smiled upon the child,
    And sung this lullaby to him,—
        This "ninna and anninia":

"When thou art older, thou shalt mind
    To traverse countries far and wide,
And thou shalt go where roses blow
    And balmy waters singing glide—
        So ninna and anninia!

"And thou shalt wear, trimmed up in points,
    A famous jacket edged in red,
And, more than that, a peakèd hat,
    All decked in gold, upon thy head—
        Ah! ninna and anninia!

"Then shalt thou carry gun and knife,
    Nor shall the soldiers bully thee;

Perchance, beset by wrong or debt,
  A mighty bandit thou shalt be—
    So ninna and anninia!

"No woman yet of our proud race
  Lived to her fourteenth year unwed;
The brazen churl that eyed a girl
  Bought her the ring or paid his head—
    So ninna and anninia!

"But once came spies (I know the thieves!)
  And brought disaster to our race;
God heard us when our fifteen men
  Were hanged within the market-place—
    But ninna and anninia!

"Good men they were, my babe, and true,—
  Right worthy fellows all, and strong;
Live thou and be for them and me
  Avenger of that deadly wrong—
    So ninna and anninia!"

LITTLE HOMER'S SLATE

AFTER dear old grandma died,
    Hunting through an oaken chest
In the attic, we espied
  What repaid our childish quest;
'Twas a homely little slate,
Seemingly of ancient date.

On its quaint and battered face
    Was the picture of a cart,
Drawn with all that awkward grace
    Which betokens childish art;
But what meant this legend, pray:
"Homer drew this yesterday"?

Mother recollected then
    What the years were fain to hide—
She was but a baby when
    Little Homer lived and died;
Forty years, so mother said,
Little Homer had been dead.

This one secret through those years
    Grandma kept from all apart,
Hallowed by her lonely tears
    And the breaking of her heart;
While each year that sped away
Seemed to her but yesterday.

So the homely little slate
    Grandma's baby's fingers pressed,
To a memory consecrate,
    Lieth in the oaken chest,
Where, unwilling we should know,
Grandma put it, years ago.

HI-SPY

STRANGE that the city thoroughfare,
  Noisy and bustling all the day,
Should with the night renounce its care
  And lend itself to children's play!

Oh, girls are girls, and boys are boys,
  And have been so since Abel's birth,
And shall be so till dolls and toys
  Are with the children swept from earth.

The selfsame sport that crowns the day
  Of many a Syrian shepherd's son,
Beguiles the little lads at play
  By night in stately Babylon.

I hear their voices in the street,
  Yet 'tis so different now from then!
Come, brother! from your winding-sheet,
  And let us two be boys again!

THE ROCK-A-BY LADY

THE Rock-a-By Lady from Hushaby street
　　Comes stealing; comes creeping;
The poppies they hang from her head to her feet,
And each hath a dream that is tiny and fleet—
She bringeth her poppies to you, my sweet,
　　When she findeth you sleeping!

There is one little dream of a beautiful drum—
　　"Rub-a-dub!" it goeth;
There is one little dream of a big sugar-plum,
And lo! thick and fast the other dreams come
Of popguns that bang, and tin tops that hum,
　　And a trumpet that bloweth!

And dollies peep out of those wee little dreams
　　With laughter and singing;
And boats go a-floating on silvery streams,
And the stars peek-a-boo with their own misty gleams
And up, up, and up, where the Mother Moon beams,
　　The fairies go winging!

Would you dream all these dreams that are tiny and fleet?
　　They'll come to you sleeping;
So shut the two eyes that are weary, my sweet,
For the Rock-a-By Lady from Hushaby street,
With poppies that hang from her head to her feet,
　　Comes stealing; comes creeping.

"BOOH!"

O N afternoons, when baby boy has had a splendid nap,
   And sits, like any monarch on his throne, in nurse's lap,
In some such wise my handkerchief I hold before my face,
And cautiously and quietly I move about the place;
Then, with a cry, I suddenly expose my face to view,
And you should hear him laugh and crow when I say "Booh!"

Sometimes the rascal tries to make believe that he is scared,
And really, when I first began, he stared, and stared, and stared;
And then his under lip came out and farther out it came,
Till mamma and the nurse agreed it was a "cruel shame"—
But now what does that same wee, toddling, lisping baby do
But laugh and kick his little heels when I say "Booh!"

He laughs and kicks his little heels in rapturous glee, and then
In shrill, despotic treble bids me "do it all aden!"
And I—of course I do it; for, as his progenitor,
It is such pretty, pleasant play as this that I am for!
And it is, oh, such fun! and I am sure that we shall rue
The time when we are both too old to play the game of "Booh!"

GARDEN AND CRADLE

W HEN our babe he goeth walking in his garden,
    Around his tinkling feet the sunbeams play;
       The posies they are good to him,
     And bow them as they should to him,
   As fareth he upon his kingly way;
      And birdlings of the wood to him
    Make music, gentle music, all the day,
When our babe he goeth walking in his garden.

When our babe he goeth swinging in his cradle,
  Then the night it looketh ever sweetly down;
    The little stars are kind to him,
    The moon she hath a mind to him
  And layeth on his head a golden crown;
    And singeth then the wind to him
  A song, the gentle song of Bethlem-town,
When our babe he goeth swinging in his cradle.

THE NIGHT WIND

HAVE you ever heard the wind go "Yooooo"?
      'Tis a pitiful sound to hear!
It seems to chill you through and through
    With a strange and speechless fear.
'Tis the voice of the night that broods outside
    When folk should be asleep,
And many and many's the time I've cried
To the darkness brooding far and wide
    Over the land and the deep:
    "Whom do you want, O lonely night,
    That you wail the long hours through?"
And the night would say in its ghostly way:
            "Yoooooooo!
            Yoooooooo!
            Yoooooooo!"

My mother told me long ago
  (When I was a little tad)
That when the night went wailing so,
  Somebody had been bad;
And then, when I was snug in bed,
  Whither I had been sent,
With the blankets pulled up round my head,
I'd think of what my mother'd said,
  And wonder what boy she meant!

And "Who's been bad to-day?" I'd ask
  Of the wind that hoarsely blew,
And the voice would say in its meaningful way:
        "Yoooooooo!
        Yoooooooo!
        Yoooooooo!"

That this was true I must allow—
  You'll not believe it, though!
Yes, though I'm quite a model now,
  I was not always so.
And if you doubt what things I say,
  Suppose you make the test;
Suppose, when you've been bad some day
And up to bed are sent away
  From mother and the rest—
Suppose you ask, "Who has been bad?"
  And then you'll hear what's true;
For the wind will moan in its ruefulest tone:
        "Yoooooooo!
        Yoooooooo!
        Yoooooooo!"

KISSING TIME

TIS when the lark goes soaring
   And the bee is at the bud,
When lightly dancing zephyrs
   Sing over field and flood;
When all sweet things in nature
   Seem joyfully achime—
'Tis then I wake my darling,
   For it is kissing time!

Go, pretty lark, a-soaring,
   And suck your sweets, O bee;
Sing, O ye winds of summer,
   Your songs to mine and me;
For with your song and rapture
   Cometh the moment when
It's half-past kissing time
   And time to kiss again!

So—so the days go fleeting
   Like golden fancies free,
And every day that cometh
   Is full of sweets for me;
And sweetest are those moments
   My darling comes to climb
Into my lap to mind me
   That it is kissing time.

Sometimes, maybe, he wanders
A heedless, aimless way—
Sometimes, maybe, he loiters
In pretty, prattling play;
But presently bethinks him
And hastens to me then,
For it's half-past kissing time
And time to kiss again!

JEST 'FORE CHRISTMAS

FATHER calls me William, sister calls me Will,
    Mother calls me Willie, but the fellers call me Bill!
Mighty glad I ain't a girl—ruther be a boy,
Without them sashes, curls, an' things, that's worn by Fauntleroy!
Love to chawnk green apples an' go swimmin' in the lake—
Hate to take the castor-ile they give for belly-ache!
'Most all the time, the whole year round, there ain't no flies on me,
But jest 'fore Christmas I'm as good as I kin be!

Got a yeller dog named Sport, sick him on the cat;
First thing she knows she doesn't know where she is at!
Got a clipper sled, an' when us kids goes out to slide,
'Long comes the grocery cart, an' we all hook a ride!
But sometimes when the grocery man is worrited an' cross,
He reaches at us with his whip, an' larrups up his hoss,
An' then I laff an' holler, "Oh, ye never teched *me!*"
But jest 'fore Christmas I'm as good as I kin be!

Gran'ma says she hopes that when I git to be a man,
I'll be a missionarer like her oldest brother, Dan,

As was et up by the cannibuls that lives in Ceylon's Isle,
Where every prospeck pleases, an' only man is vile!
But gran'ma she has never been to see a Wild West show,
Nor read the Life of Daniel Boone, or else I guess she'd know
That Buff'lo Bill an' cow-boys is good enough for me!
Excep' jest 'fore Christmas, when I'm good as I kin be!

And then old Sport he hangs around, so solemn-like an' still,
His eyes they seem a-sayin': "What's the matter, little Bill?"
The old cat sneaks down off her perch an' wonders what's become
Of them two enemies of hern that used to make things hum!
But I am so perlite an' 'tend so earnestly to biz,
That mother says to father: "How improved our Willie is!"
But father, havin' been a boy hisself, suspicions me
When, jest 'fore Christmas, I'm as good as I kin be!

For Christmas, with its lots an' lots of candies, cakes, an' toys,
Was made, they say, for proper kids, an' not for naughty boys:
So wash yer face an' bresh yer hair, an' mind yer p's and q's,
An' don't bust out yer pantaloons, and don't wear out yer shoes;
Say "Yessum" to the ladies, an' "Yessur" to the men,
An' when they's company, don't pass yer plate for pie again;
But, thinkin' of the things yer'd like to see upon that tree,
Jest 'fore Christmas be as good as yer kin be!

BEARD AND BABY

I SAY, as one who never feared
   The wrath of a subscriber's bullet,
I pity him who has a beard
   But has no little girl to pull it!

When wife and I have finished tea,
   Our baby woos me with her prattle,
And, perching proudly on my knee,
   She gives my petted whiskers battle.

With both her hands she tugs away,
   While scolding at me kind o' spiteful;
You'll not believe me when I say
   I find the torture quite delightful!

No other would presume, I ween,
   To trifle with this hirsute wonder,
Else would I rise in vengeful mien
   And rend his vandal frame asunder!

But when *her* baby fingers pull
   This glossy, sleek, and silky treasure,
My cup of happiness is full—
   I fairly glow with pride and pleasure!

And, sweeter still, through all the day
   I seem to hear her winsome prattle—
I seem to feel her hands at play,
   As though they gave me sportive battle.

Yes, heavenly music seems to steal
   Where thought of her forever lingers,
And round my heart I always feel
   The twining of her dimpled fingers!

THE DINKEY-BIRD

IN an ocean, 'way out yonder
  (As all sapient people know),
Is the land of Wonder-Wander,
  Whither children love to go;
It's their playing, romping, swinging,
  That give great joy to me
While the Dinkey-Bird goes singing
  In the amfalula tree!

There the gum-drops grow like cherries,
  And taffy's thick as peas—
Caramels you pick like berries
  When, and where, and how you please;
Big red sugar-plums are clinging
  To the cliffs beside that sea
Where the Dinkey-Bird is singing
  In the amfalula tree.

So when children shout and scamper
  And make merry all the day,
When there's naught to put a damper
  To the ardor of their play;
When I hear their laughter ringing,
  Then I'm sure as sure can be
That the Dinkey-Bird is singing
  In the amfalula tree.

For the Dinkey-Bird's bravuras
  And staccatos are so sweet—
His roulades, appoggiaturas,
  And robustos so complete,
That the youth of every nation—
  Be they near or far away—

Have especial delectation
In that gladsome roundelay.

Their eyes grow bright and brighter
Their lungs begin to crow,
Their hearts get light and lighter,
And their cheeks are all aglow;
For an echo cometh bringing
The news to all and me,
That the Dinkey-Bird is singing
In the amfalula tree.

I'm sure you like to go there
To see your feathered friend—
And so many goodies grow there
You would like to comprehend!
Speed, little dreams, your winging
To that land across the sea
Where the Dinkey-Bird is singing
In the amfalula tree!

THE DRUM

I'M a beautiful red, red drum,
And I train with the soldier boys;
As up the street we come,
Wonderful is our noise!
There's Tom, and Jim, and Phil,
And Dick, and Nat, and Fred,
While Widow Cutler's Bill
And I march on ahead,
With a r-r-rat-tat-tat

And a tum-titty-um-tum-tum—
Oh, there's bushels of fun in that
For boys with a little red drum!

The Injuns came last night
  While the soldiers were abed,
And they gobbled a Chinese kite
  And off to the woods they fled!
The woods are the cherry-trees
  Down in the orchard lot,
And the soldiers are marching to seize
  The booty the Injuns got.
With tum-titty-um-tum-tum,
  And r-r-rat-tat-tat,
When soldiers marching come
  Injuns had better scat!

Step up there, little Fred,
  And, Charley, have a mind!
Jim is as far ahead
  As you two are behind!
Ready with gun and sword
  Your valorous work to do—
Yonder the Injun horde
  Are lying in wait for you.
And their hearts go pitapat
  When they hear the soldiers come
With a r-r-rat-tat-tat
  And a tum-titty-um-tum-tum!

Course it's all in play!
   The skulking Injun crew
That hustled the kite away
   Are little white boys, like you!
But "honest" or "just in fun,"
   It is all the same to me;
And, when the battle is won,
   Home once again march we
With a r-r-rat-tat-tat
   And tum-titty-um-tum-tum;
And there's glory enough in that
   For the boys with their little red drum!

THE DEAD BABE

LAST night, as my dear babe lay dead,
   In agony I knelt and said:
      "O God! what have I done,
Or in what wise offended Thee,
That Thou shouldst take away from me
      My little son?

"Upon the thousand useless lives,
Upon the guilt that vaunting thrives,
      Thy wrath were better spent!
Why shouldst Thou take my little son—
Why shouldst Thou vent Thy wrath upon
      This innocent?"

Last night, as my dear babe lay dead,
Before mine eyes the vision spread

Of things that *might* have been:
Licentious riot, cruel strife,
Forgotten prayers, a wasted life
    Dark red with sin!

Then, with sweet music in the air,
I saw another vision there:
    A Shepherd in whose keep
A little lamb—my little child!
Of worldly wisdom undefiled,
    Lay fast asleep!

Last night, as my dear babe lay dead,
In those two messages I read
    A wisdom manifest;
And though my arms be childless now,
I am content—to Him I bow
    Who knoweth best.

THE HAPPY HOUSEHOLD

IT'S when the birds go piping and the daylight slowly breaks,
  That, clamoring for his dinner, our precious baby wakes;
Then it's sleep no more for baby, and it's sleep no more for me,
For, when he wants his dinner, why it's dinner it must be!
And of that lacteal fluid he partakes with great ado,
      While gran'ma laughs,
      And gran'pa laughs,
      And wife, she laughs,
      And I—well, *I* laugh, *too!*

You'd think, to see us carrying on about that little tad,
That, like as not, that baby was the first we'd ever had;
But, sakes alive! he isn't, yet we people make a fuss
As if the only baby in the world had come to *us!*
And, morning, noon, and night-time, whatever he may do,
                    Gran'ma, she laughs,
                    Gran'pa, he laughs,
                    Wife, she laughs,
                    And *I*, of course, laugh, too!

But once—a likely spell ago—when that poor little chick
From teething or from some such ill of infancy fell sick,
You wouldn't know us people as the same that went about
A-feelin' good all over, just to hear him crow and shout;
And, though the doctor poohed our fears and said he'd pull him
        through,
                    Old gran'ma cried,
                    And gran'pa cried,
                    And wife, she cried,
                    And I—yes, *I* cried, *too!*

It makes us all feel good to have a baby on the place,
With his everlastin' crowing and his dimpling, dumpling face;
The patter of his pinky feet makes music everywhere,
And when he shakes those fists of his, good-by to every care!
No matter *what* our trouble is, when *he* begins to *coo*,
                    Old gran'ma laughs,
                    And gran'pa laughs,
                    Wife, she laughs,
                    And I—you bet, *I* laugh, *too!*

SO, SO, ROCK-A-BY SO!

So, so, rock-a-by so!
  Off to the garden where dreamikins grow;
And here is a kiss on your winkyblink eyes,
  And here is a kiss on your dimpledown cheek
And here is a kiss for the treasure that lies
In the beautiful garden way up in the skies
  Which you seek.
Now mind these three kisses wherever you go—
So, so, rock-a-by so!

There's one little fumfay who lives there, I know,
For he dances all night where the dreamikins grow;
I send him this kiss on your droopydrop eyes,
  I send him this kiss on your rosyred cheek.
And here is a kiss for the dream that shall rise
When the fumfay shall dance in those far-away skies
  Which you seek.
Be sure that you pay those three kisses you owe—
So, so, rock-a-by so!

And, by-low, as you rock-a-by go
Don't forget mother who loveth you so!
And here is her kiss on your weepydeep eyes,
  And here is her kiss on your peachypink cheek,
And here is her kiss for the dreamland that lies
Like a babe on the breast of those far-away skies
  Which you seek—
The blinkywink garden where dreamikins grow—
So, so, rock-a-by so!

THE DUEL

THE gingham dog and the calico cat
    Side by side on the table sat;
  'Twas half-past twelve, and (what do you think!)
Nor one nor t'other had slept a wink!
    The old Dutch clock and the Chinese plate
    Appeared to know as sure as fate
There was going to be a terrible spat.
       (I wasn't there; I simply state
       What was told to me by the Chinese plate!)

The gingham dog went "bow-wow-wow!"
And the calico cat replied "mee-ow!"
The air was littered, an hour or so,
With bits of gingham and calico,
    While the old Dutch clock in the chimney-place
    Up with its hands before its face,
For it always dreaded a family row!
       (Now mind: I'm only telling you
       What the old Dutch clock declares is true!)

The Chinese plate looked very blue,
And wailed, "Oh, dear! what shall we do!"
But the gingham dog and the calico cat
Wallowed this way and tumbled that,
Employing every tooth and claw
In the awfullest way you ever saw—
And, oh! how the gingham and calico flew!
       (Don't fancy I exaggerate—
       I got my news from the Chinese plate!)

Next morning, where the two had sat
They found no trace of dog or cat;
And some folks think unto this day

That burglars stole that pair away!
But the truth about the cat and pup
Is this: they ate each other up!
Now what do you really think of that!
(The old Dutch clock it told me so,
And that is how I came to know.)

GOOD-CHILDREN STREET

THERE'S a dear little home in Good-Children street—
My heart turneth fondly to-day
Where tinkle of tongues and patter of feet
Make sweetest of music at play;
Where the sunshine of love illumines each face
And warms every heart in that old-fashioned place.

For dear little children go romping about
With dollies and tin tops and drums,
And, my! how they frolic and scamper and shout
Till bedtime too speedily comes!
Oh, days they are golden and days they are fleet
With little folk living in Good-Children street.

See, here comes an army with guns painted red,
And swords, caps, and plumes of all sorts;
The captain rides gayly and proudly ahead
On a stick-horse that prances and snorts!
Oh, legions of soldiers you're certain to meet—
Nice make-believe soldiers—in Good-Children street.

And yonder Odette wheels her dolly about—
Poor dolly! I'm sure she is ill,
For one of her blue china eyes has dropped out
And her voice is asthmatic'ly shrill.

Then, too, I observe she is minus her feet,
Which causes much sorrow in Good-Children street.

'Tis so the dear children go romping about
    With dollies and banners and drums,
And I venture to say they are sadly put out
    When an end to their jubilee comes:
Oh, days they are golden and days they are fleet
With little folk living in Good-Children street!

But when falleth night over river and town,
    Those little folk vanish from sight,
And an angel all white from the sky cometh down
    And guardeth the babes through the night,
And singeth her lullabies tender and sweet
To the dear little people in Good-Children street.

Though elsewhere the world be o'erburdened with care,
    Though poverty fall to my lot,
Though toil and vexation be always my share,
    What care I—they trouble me not!
This thought maketh life ever joyous and sweet:
There's a dear little home in Good-Children street.

THE DELECTABLE BALLAD
OF THE WALLER LOT

UP yonder in Buena Park
    There is a famous spot,
In legend and in history
    Yclept the Waller Lot.

There children play in daytime
    And lovers stroll by dark,
For 'tis the goodliest trysting-place
    In all Buena Park.

Once on a time that beauteous maid,
    Sweet little Sissy Knott,
Took out her pretty doll to walk
    Within the Waller Lot.

While thus she fared, from Ravenswood
    Came Injuns o'er the plain,
And seized upon that beauteous maid
    And rent her doll in twain.

Oh, 'twas a piteous thing to hear
    Her lamentations wild;
She tore her golden curls and cried:
    "My child! My child! My child!"

Alas, what cared those Injun chiefs
    How bitterly wailed she?
They never had been mothers,
    And they could not hope to be!

"Have done with tears," they rudely quoth,
    And then they bound her hands;
For they proposed to take her off
    To distant border lands.

But, joy! from Mr. Eddy's barn
  Doth Willie Clow behold
The sight that makes his hair rise up
  And all his blood run cold.

He put his fingers in his mouth
  And whistled long and clear,
And presently a goodly horde
  Of cow-boys did appear.

Cried Willie Clow: "My comrades bold,
  Haste to the Waller Lot,
And rescue from that Injun band
  Our charming Sissy Knott!

"Spare neither Injun buck nor squaw,
  But smite them hide and hair!
Spare neither sex nor age nor size,
  And no condition spare!"

Then sped that cow-boy band away,
  Full of revengeful wrath,
And Kendall Evans rode ahead
  Upon a hickory lath.

And next came gallant Dady Field
  And Willie's brother Kent,
The Eddy boys and Robbie James,
  On murderous purpose bent.

For they were much beholden to
  That maid—in sooth, the lot
Were very, very much in love
  With charming Sissy Knott.

What wonder? She was beauty's queen,
    And good beyond compare;
Moreover, it was known she was
    Her wealthy father's heir!

Now when the Injuns saw that band
    They trembled with affright,
And yet they thought the cheapest thing
    To do was stay and fight.

So sturdily they stood their ground,
    Nor would their prisoner yield,
Despite the wrath of Willie Clow
    And gallant Dady Field.

Oh, never fiercer battle raged
    Upon the Waller Lot,
And never blood more freely flowed
    Than flowed for Sissy Knott!

An Injun chief of monstrous size
    Got Kendall Evans down,
And Robbie James was soon o'erthrown
    By one of great renown.

And Dady Field was sorely done,
    And Willie Clow was hurt,
And all that gallant cow-boy band
    Lay wallowing in the dirt.

But still they strove with might and main
    Till all the Waller Lot
Was strewn with hair and gouts of gore—
    All, all for Sissy Knott!

Then cried the maiden in despair:
  "Alas, I sadly fear
The battle and my hopes are lost,
  Unless some help appear!"

Lo, as she spoke, she saw afar
  The rescuer looming up—
The pride of all Buena Park,
  Clow's famous yellow pup!

"Now, sick 'em, Don," the maiden cried,
  "Now, sick 'em, Don!" cried she;
Obedient Don at once complied—
  As ordered, so did he.

He sicked 'em all so passing well
  That, overcome by fright,
The Indian horde gave up the fray
  And safety sought in flight.

They ran and ran and ran and ran
  O'er valley, plain, and hill;
And if they are not walking now,
  Why, then, they're running still.

The cow-boys rose up from the dust
  With faces black and blue;
"Remember, beauteous maid," said they,
  "We've bled and died for you!

"And though we suffer grievously,
  We gladly hail the lot
That brings us toils and pains and wounds
  For charming Sissy Knott!"

But Sissy Knott still wailed and wept,
    And still her fate reviled;
For who could patch her dolly up—
    Who, who could mend her child?

Then out her doting mother came,
    And soothed her daughter then;
"Grieve not, my darling, I will sew
    Your dolly up again!"

Joy soon succeeded unto grief,
    And tears were soon dried up,
And dignities were heaped upon
    Clow's noble yellow pup.

Him all that goodly company
    Did as deliverer hail—
They tied a ribbon round his neck,
    Another round his tail.

And every anniversary day
    Upon the Waller Lot
They celebrate the victory won
    For charming Sissy Knott.

And I, the poet of these folk,
    Am ordered to compile
This truly famous history
    In good old ballad style.

Which having done as to have earned
    The sweet rewards of fame,
In what same style I did begin
    I now shall end the same.

So let us sing: Long live the King,
    Long live the Queen and Jack,
    Long live the ten-spot and the ace,
      And also all the pack.

THE FLY-AWAY HORSE

OH, a wonderful horse is the Fly-Away Horse—
    Perhaps you have seen him before;
Perhaps, while you slept, his shadow has swept
    Through the moonlight that floats on the floor.
For it's only at night, when the stars twinkle bright,
    That the Fly-Away Horse, with a neigh
And a pull at his rein and a toss of his mane,
    Is up on his heels and away!
        The Moon in the sky,
        As he gallopeth by,
    Cries: "Oh! what a marvellous sight!"
        And the Stars in dismay
        Hide their faces away
    In the lap of old Grandmother Night.

It is yonder, out yonder, the Fly-Away Horse
    Speedeth ever and ever away—
Over meadows and lanes, over mountains and plains,
    Over streamlets that sing at their play;
And over the sea like a ghost sweepeth he,
    While the ships they go sailing below,
And he speedeth so fast that the men at the mast
    Adjudge him some portent of woe.
        "What ho there!" they cry,
        As he flourishes by

With a whisk of his beautiful tail;
  And the fish in the sea
  Are as scared as can be,
From the nautilus up to the whale!

And the Fly-Away Horse seeks those far-away lands
  You little folk dream of at night—
Where candy-trees grow, and honey-brooks flow,
  And corn-fields with popcorn are white;
And the beasts in the wood are ever so good
  To children who visit them there—
What glory astride of a lion to ride,
  Or to wrestle around with a bear!
    The monkeys, they say:
    "Come on, let us play,"
  And they frisk in the cocoanut-trees:
    While the parrots, that cling
    To the peanut-vines, sing
  Or converse with comparative ease!

Off! scamper to bed—you shall ride him to-night!
  For, as soon as you've fallen asleep,
With a jubilant neigh he shall bear you away
  Over forest and hillside and deep!
But tell us, my dear, all you see and you hear
  In those beautiful lands over there,
Where the Fly-Away Horse wings his far-away course
  With the wee one consigned to his care.
    Then grandma will cry
    In amazement: "Oh, my!"
  And she'll think it could never be so;
    And only we two
    Shall know it is true—
  You and I, little precious! shall know!

THE STORK

LAST night the Stork came stalking,
   And, Stork, beneath your wing
Lay, lapped in dreamless slumber,
   The tiniest little thing!
From Babyland, out yonder
   Beside a silver sea,
You brought a priceless treasure
   As gift to mine and me!

Last night my dear one listened—
   And, wife, you knew the cry—
The dear old Stork has sought our home
   A many times gone by!
And in your gentle bosom
   I found the pretty thing
That from the realm out yonder
   Our friend the Stork did bring.

Last night a babe awakened,
   And, babe, how strange and new
Must seem the home and people
   The Stork has brought you to;
And yet methinks you like them—
   You neither stare nor weep,
But closer to my dear one
   You cuddle, and you sleep!

Last night my heart grew fonder—
   O happy heart of mine,
Sing of the inspirations
   That round my pathway shine!
And sing your sweetest love-song
   To this dear nestling wee
The Stork from 'Way-Out-Yonder
   Hath brought to mine and me!

THE BOTTLE TREE

A BOTTLE TREE bloometh in Winkyway land—
   Heigh-ho for a bottle, I say!
A snug little berth in that ship I demand
   That rocketh the Bottle-Tree babies away
   Where the Bottle Tree bloometh by night and by day
And reacheth its fruit to each wee, dimpled hand;
   You take of that fruit as much as you list,
   For colic's a nuisance that doesn't exist!
So cuddle me close, and cuddle me fast,
   And cuddle me snug in my cradle away,
For I hunger and thirst for that precious repast—
   Heigh-ho for a bottle, I say!

The Bottle Tree bloometh by night and by day!
   Heigh-ho for Winkyway land!
And Bottle-Tree fruit (as I've heard people say)
   Makes bellies of Bottle-Tree babies expand—
   And that is a trick I would fain understand!
Heigh-ho for a bottle to-day!
   And heigh-ho for a bottle to-night—
   A bottle of milk that is creamy and white!
So cuddle me close, and cuddle me fast,
   And cuddle me snug in my cradle away,
For I hunger and thirst for that precious repast—
   Heigh-ho for a bottle, I say!

GOOGLY-GOO

OF mornings, bright and early,
   When the lark is on the wing
And the robin in the maple
   Hops from her nest to sing,

From yonder cheery chamber
　　Cometh a mellow coo—
'Tis the sweet, persuasive treble
　　Of my little Googly-Goo!

The sunbeams hear his music,
　　And they seek his little bed,
And they dance their prettiest dances
　　Round his golden curly head:
Schottisches, galops, minuets,
　　Gavottes and waltzes, too,
Dance they unto the music
　　Of my googling Googly-Goo.

My heart—my heart it leapeth
　　To hear that treble tone;
What music like *thy* music,
　　My darling and mine own!
And patiently—yes, cheerfully
　　I toil the long day through—
My labor seemeth lightened
　　By the song of Googly-Goo!

I may not see his antics,
　　Nor kiss his dimpled cheek:
I may not smooth the tresses
　　The sunbeams love to seek;
It mattereth not—the echo
　　Of his sweet, persuasive coo
Recurreth to remind me
　　Of my little Googly-goo.

And when I come at evening,
　　I stand without the door
And patiently I listen
　　For that dear sound once more;

And oftentimes I wonder,
"Oh, God! what should I do
If any ill should happen
To my little Googly-Goo!"

Then in affright I call him—
I hear his gleeful shouts!
Begone, ye dread forebodings—
Begone, ye killing doubts!
For, with my arms about him,
My heart warms through and through
With the oogling and the googling
Of my little Googly-Goo!

THE BENCH-LEGGED FYCE

SPEAKIN' of dorgs, my bench-legged fyce
Hed most o' the virtues, an' nary a vice.
Some folks called him Sooner, a name that arose
From his predisposition to chronic repose;
But, rouse his ambition, he couldn't be beat—
Yer bet yer he got thar on all his four feet!

Mos' dorgs hez some forte—like huntin' an' such,
But the sports o' the field didn't bother *him* much;
Wuz just a plain dorg, an' contented to be
On peaceable terms with the neighbors an' me;
Used to fiddle an' squirm, and grunt "Oh, how nice!"
When I tickled the back of that bench-legged fyce!

He wuz long in the bar'l, like a fyce oughter be;
His color wuz yaller as ever you see;
His tail, curlin' upward, wuz long, loose, an' slim—
When he didn't wag *it*, why, the tail it wagged *him!*
His legs wuz so crooked, my bench-legged pup
Wuz as tall settin' down as he wuz standin' up!

He'd lie by the stove of a night an' regret
The various vittles an' things he had et;
When a stranger, most likely a tramp, come along,
He'd lift up his voice in significant song—
You wondered, by gum! how there ever wuz space
In that bosom o' his'n to hold so much bass!

Of daytimes he'd sneak to the road an' lie down,
An' tackle the country dorgs comin' to town;
By common consent he wuz boss in St. Joe,
For what he took hold of he never let go!
An' a dude that come courtin' our girl left a slice
Of his white flannel suit with our bench-legged fyce!

He wuz good to us kids—when we pulled at his fur
Or twisted his tail he would never demur;
He seemed to enjoy all our play an' our chaff,
For his tongue 'u'd hang out an' he'd laff an' he'd laff;
An' once, when the Hobart boy fell through the ice,
He wuz drug clean ashore by that bench-legged fyce!

We all hev our choice, an' you, like the rest,
Allow that the dorg which you've got is the best;
I wouldn't give much for the boy 'at grows up
With no friendship subsistin' 'tween him an' a pup!
When a fellow gits old—I tell you it's nice
To think of his youth and his bench-legged fyce!

To think of the springtime 'way back in St. Joe—
Of the peach-trees abloom an' the daisies ablow;
To think of the play in the medder an' grove,
When little legs wrassled an' little han's strove;
To think of the loyalty, valor, an' truth
Of the friendships that hallow the season of youth!

LITTLE MISS BRAG

LITTLE Miss Brag has much to say
    To the rich little lady from over the way,
And the rich little lady puts out a lip
As she looks at her own white, dainty slip,
And wishes that *she* could wear a gown
As pretty as gingham of faded brown!
For little Miss Brag she lays much stress
On the privileges of a gingham dress—
            "Aha,
            Oho!"

The rich little lady from over the way
Has beautiful dolls in vast array;
Yet she envies the raggedy home-made doll
She hears our little Miss Brag extol.
For the raggedy doll can fear no hurt
From wet, or heat, or tumble, or dirt!
Her nose is inked, and her mouth is, too,
And one eye's black and the other's blue—
            "Aha,
            Oho!"

The rich little lady goes out to ride
With footmen standing up outside,
Yet wishes that, sometimes, after dark
Her father would trundle *her* in the park;—
That, sometimes, *her* mother would sing the things
Little Miss Brag says *her* mother sings
When through the attic window streams
The moonlight full of golden dreams—
"Aha,
Oho!"

Yes, little Miss Brag has much to say
To the rich little lady from over the way;
And yet who knows but from her heart
Often the bitter sighs upstart—
Uprise to lose their burn and sting
In the grace of the tongue that loves to sing
Praise of the treasures all its own!
So I've come to love that treble tone—
"Aha,
Oho!"

THE HUMMING-TOP

THE top it hummeth a sweet, sweet song
    To my dear little boy at play—
Merrily singeth all day long,
    As it spinneth and spinneth away.
            And my dear little boy
            He laugheth with joy
When he heareth the monotone
            Of that busy thing
            That loveth to sing
The song that is all its own.

Hold fast the string and wind it tight,
    That the song be loud and clear;
Now hurl the top with all your might
    Upon the banquette here;
            And straight from the string
            The joyous thing
Boundeth and spinneth along,
            And it whirrs and it chirrs
            And it birrs and it purrs
Ever its pretty song.

Will ever my dear little boy grow old,
    As some have grown before?
Will ever his heart feel faint and cold,
    When he heareth the songs of yore?
            Will ever this toy
            Of my dear little boy,
When the years have worn away,
            Sing sad and low
            Of the long ago,
As it singeth to me to-day?

LADY BUTTON-EYES

WHEN the busy day is done,
And my weary little one
Rocketh gently to and fro;
When the night winds softly blow,
When the crickets in the glen
Chirp and chirp and chirp again;
When upon the haunted green
Fairies dance around their queen—
Then from yonder misty skies
Cometh Lady Button-Eyes.

Through the murk and mist and gloam,
To our quiet, cosey home,
Where to singing, sweet and low,
Rocks a cradle to and fro;
Where the clock's dull monotone
Telleth of the day that's done;
Where the moonbeams hover o'er
Playthings sleeping on the floor—
Where my weary wee one lies
Cometh Lady Button-Eyes.

Cometh like a fleeting ghost
From some distant eerie coast;
Never footfall can you hear
As that spirit fareth near—
Never whisper, never word
From that shadow-queen is heard.
In ethereal raiment dight,
From the realm of fay and sprite
In the depth of yonder skies
Cometh Lady Button-Eyes.

Layeth she her hands upon
My dear weary little one,
And those white hands overspread
Like a veil the curly head,
Seem to fondle and caress
Every little silken tress;
Then she smooths the eyelids down
Over those two eyes of brown—
In such soothing, tender wise
Cometh Lady Button-Eyes.

Dearest, feel upon your brow
That caressing magic now;
For the crickets in the glen
Chirp and chirp and chirp again,
While upon the haunted green
Fairies dance around their queen,
And the moonbeams hover o'er
Playthings sleeping on the floor—
Hush, my sweet! from yonder skies
Cometh Lady Button-Eyes!

THE RIDE TO BUMPVILLE

PLAY that my knee was a calico mare
　　Saddled and bridled for Bumpville;
Leap to the back of this steed, if you dare,
　　And gallop away to Bumpville!
I hope you'll be sure to sit fast in your seat,
For this calico mare is prodigiously fleet,
And many adventures you're likely to meet
　　As you journey along to Bumpville.

This calico mare both gallops and trots
    While whisking you off to Bumpville;
She paces, she shies, and she stumbles, in spots,
    In the tortuous road to Bumpville;
And sometimes this strangely mercurial steed
Will suddenly stop and refuse to proceed,
Which, all will admit, is vexatious indeed,
    When one is en route to Bumpville!

She's scared of the cars when the engine goes "Toot!"
    Down by the crossing at Bumpville;
You'd better look out for that treacherous brute
    Bearing you off to Bumpville!
With a snort she rears up on her hindermost heels,
And executes jigs and Virginia reels—
Words fail to explain how embarrassed one feels
    Dancing so wildly to Bumpville!

It's bumpytybump and it's jiggytyjog,
    Journeying on to Bumpville;
It's over the hilltop and down through the bog
    You ride on your way to Bumpville;
It's rattletybang over boulder and stump,
There are rivers to ford, there are fences to jump,
And the corduroy road it goes bumpytybump,
    Mile after mile to Bumpville!

Perhaps you'll observe it's no easy thing
    Making the journey to Bumpville,
So I think, on the whole, it were prudent to bring
    An end to this ride to Bumpville;
For, though she has uttered no protest or plaint,
The calico mare must be blowing and faint—
What's more to the point, I'm blowed if I ain't!
    So play we have got to Bumpville!

THE BROOK

I LOOKED in the brook and saw a face—
   Heigh-ho, but a child was I!
There were rushes and willows in that place,
   And they clutched at the brook as the brook ran by;
And the brook it ran its own sweet way,
As a child doth run in heedless play,
And as it ran I heard it say:
      "Hasten with me
       To the roistering sea
That is wroth with the flame of the morning sky!"

I look in the brook and see a face—
   Heigh-ho, but the years go by!
The rushes are dead in the old-time place,
   And the willows I knew when a child was I.
And the brook it seemeth to me to say,
As ever it stealeth on its way—
Solemnly now, and not in play:
      "Oh, come with me
       To the slumbrous sea
That is gray with the peace of the evening sky!"

Heigh-ho, but the years go by—
I would to God that a child were I!

PICNIC-TIME

IT'S June ag'in, an' in my soul I feel the fillin' joy
  That's sure to come this time o' year to every little boy;
For, every June, the Sunday-schools at picnics may be seen,
Where "fields beyont the swellin' floods stand dressed in livin'
        green";
Where little girls are skeered to death with spiders, bugs, and ants,
An' little boys get grass-stains on their go-to-meetin' pants.
It's June ag'in, an' with it all what happiness is mine—
There's goin' to be a picnic, an' I'm goin' to jine!

One year I jined the Baptists, an' goodness! how it rained!
(But grampa says that that's the way "baptizo" is explained.)
And once I jined the 'Piscopils an' had a heap o' fun—
But the boss of all the picnics was the Presbyteriun!
They had so many puddin's, sallids, sandwidges, an' pies,
That a feller wisht his stummick was as hungry as his eyes!
Oh, yes, the eatin' Presbyteriuns give yer is so fine
That when *they* have a picnic, you bet *I'm* goin' to jine!

But at this time the Methodists have special claims on me,
For they're goin' to give a picnic on the 21st, D. V.;
Why should a liberal Universalist like me object
To share the joys of fellowship with every friendly sect?
However het'rodox their articles of faith elsewise may be,
Their doctrine of fried chick'n is a savin' grace to me!
So on the 21st of June, the weather bein' fine,
They're goin' to give a picnic, and I'm goin' to jine!

SHUFFLE-SHOON AND AMBER-LOCKS

SHUFFLE-SHOON and Amber-Locks
    Sit together, building blocks;
        Shuffle-Shoon is old and gray,
            Amber-Locks a little child,
        But together at their play
            Age and Youth are reconciled,
And with sympathetic glee
Build their castles fair to see.

"When I grow to be a man"
(So the wee one's prattle ran),
    "I shall build a castle so—
        With a gateway broad and grand;
    Here a pretty vine shall grow,
        There a soldier guard shall stand;
And the tower shall be so high,
Folks will wonder, by and by!"

Shuffle-Shoon quoth: "Yes, I know;
Thus I builded long ago!
    Here a gate and there a wall,
        Here a window, there a door;
    Here a steeple wondrous tall
        Riseth ever more and more!
But the years have levelled low
What I builded long ago!"

So they gossip at their play,
Heedless of the fleeting day;
    One speaks of the Long Ago
        Where his dead hopes buried lie;
    One with chubby cheeks aglow
        Prattleth of the By and By;
Side by side, they build their blocks—
Shuffle-Shoon and Amber-Locks.

THE SHUT-EYE TRAIN

COME, my little one, with me!
　　There are wondrous sights to see
　As the evening shadows fall;
　In your pretty cap and gown,
　　　　Don't detain
　　　　The Shut-Eye train—
　"Ting-a-ling!" the bell it goeth,
　"Toot-toot!" the whistle bloweth,
And we hear the warning call:
"All aboard for Shut-Eye Town!"

Over hill and over plain
Soon will speed the Shut-Eye train!
　Through the blue where bloom the stars
　And the Mother Moon looks down
　　　　We'll away
　　　　To land of Fay—
　Oh, the sights that we shall see there!
　Come, my little one, with me there—
'Tis a goodly train of cars—
All aboard for Shut-Eye Town!

Swifter than a wild bird's flight,
Through the realms of fleecy light
　We shall speed and speed away!
　Let the Night in envy frown—
　　　　What care we
　　　　How wroth she be!
　To the Balow-land above us,
　To the Balow-folk who love us,
Let us hasten while we may—
All aboard for Shut-Eye Town!

Shut-Eye Town is passing fair—
Golden dreams await us there;
    We shall dream those dreams, my dear,
    Till the Mother Moon goes down—
            See unfold
            Delights untold!
    And in those mysterious places
    We shall see beloved faces
And beloved voices hear
In the grace of Shut-Eye Town.

Heavy are your eyes, my sweet,
Weary are your little feet—
    Nestle closer up to me
    In your pretty cap and gown;
            Don't detain
            The Shut-Eye train!
    "Ting-a-ling!" the bell it goeth,
    "Toot-toot!" the whistle bloweth,
Oh, the sights that we shall see!
All aboard for Shut-Eye Town!

LITTLE-OH-DEAR

SEE, what a wonderful garden is here,
Planted and trimmed for my Little-Oh-Dear!
Posies so gaudy and grass of such brown—
Search ye the country and hunt ye the town
And never ye'll meet with a garden so queer
As this one I've made for my Little-Oh-Dear!

Marigolds white and buttercups blue,
Lilies all dabbled with honey and dew,
The cactus that trails over trellis and wall,
Roses and pansies and violets—all
Make proper obeisance and reverent cheer
When into her garden steps Little-Oh-Dear.

And up at the top of that lavender-tree
A silver-bird singeth as only can she;
For, ever and only, she singeth the song
"I love you—I love you!" the happy day long;—
Then the echo—the echo that smiteth me here!
"I love you, I love you," my Little-Oh-Dear!

The garden may wither, the silver-bird fly—
But what careth my little precious, or I?
From her pathway of flowers that in springtime upstart
She walketh the tenderer way in my heart
And, oh, it is always the summer-time *here*
With that song of "I love you," my Little-Oh-Dear!

SWING HIGH AND SWING LOW

SWING high and swing low
  While the breezes they blow—
It's off for a sailor thy father would go;
And it's here in the harbor, in sight of the sea,
He hath left his wee babe with my song and with me:
  "Swing high and swing low
  While the breezes they blow!"

Swing high and swing low
  While the breezes they blow—
It's oh for the waiting as weary days go!
And it's oh for the heartache that smiteth me when
I sing my song over and over again:
  "Swing high and swing low
  While the breezes they blow!"

"Swing high and swing low"—
  The sea singeth so,
And it waileth anon in its ebb and its flow;
And a sleeper sleeps on to that song of the sea
Nor recketh he ever of mine or of me!
  "Swing high and swing low
  While the breezes they blow—
  'Twas off for a sailor thy father would go!"

WHEN I WAS A BOY

UP in the attic where I slept
 When I was a boy, a little boy,
In through the lattice the moonlight crept,
Bringing a tide of dreams that swept
Over the low, red trundle-bed,
Bathing the tangled curly head,
While moonbeams played at hide-and-seek
With the dimples on the sun-browned cheek—
 When I was a boy, a little boy!

And oh! the dreams—the dreams I dreamed!
 When I was a boy, a little boy!
For the grace that through the lattice streamed
Over my folded eyelids seemed
To have the gift of prophecy,
And to bring me glimpses of times to be
When manhood's clarion seemed to call—
Ah! *that* was the sweetest dream of all,
 When I was a boy, a little boy!

I'd like to sleep where I used to sleep
 When I was a boy, a little boy!
For in at the lattice the moon would peep,
Bringing her tide of dreams to sweep
The crosses and griefs of the years away
From the heart that is weary and faint to-day;
And those dreams should give me back again
A peace I have never known since then—
 When I was a boy, a little boy!

AT PLAY

PLAY that you are mother dear,
　　And play that papa is your beau;
Play that we sit in the corner here,
　Just as we used to, long ago.
Playing so, we lovers two
　Are just as happy as we can be,
And I'll say "I love you" to you,
　And you say "I love you" to me!
"I love you" we both shall say,
All in earnest and all in play.

Or, play that you are that other one
　That some time came, and went away;
And play that the light of years agone
　Stole into my heart again to-day!
Playing that you are the one I knew
　In the days that never again may be,
I'll say "I love you" to you,
　And you say "I love you" to me!
"I love you!" my heart shall say
To the ghost of the past come back to-day!

Or, play that you.sought this nestling-place
　For your own sweet self, with that dual guise
Of your pretty mother in your face
　And the look of that other in your eyes!
So the dear old loves shall live anew
　As I hold my darling on my knee,
And I'll say "I love you" to you,
　And you say "I love you" to me!
Oh, many a strange, true thing we say
And do when we pretend to play!

A VALENTINE

G O, Cupid, and my sweetheart tell
   I love her well.
Yes, though she tramples on my heart
And rends that bleeding thing apart;
And though she rolls a scornful eye
On doting me when I go by;
And though she scouts at everything
As tribute unto her I bring—
Apple, banana, caramel—
Haste, Cupid, to my love and tell,
In spite of all, I love her well!

And further say I have a sled
Cushioned in blue and painted red!
The groceryman has promised I
Can "hitch" whenever he goes by—
Go, tell her that, and, furthermore,
Apprise my sweetheart that a score
Of other little girls implore
The boon of riding on that sled
Painted and hitched, as aforesaid;—
And tell her, Cupid, only she
Shall ride upon that sled with me!
Tell her this all, and further tell
   I love her well.

LITTLE ALL-ALONEY

LITTLE ALL–ALONEY's feet
  Pitter-patter in the hall,
And his mother runs to meet
And to kiss her toddling sweet,
  Ere perchance he fall.
He is, oh, so weak and small!
    Yet what danger shall he fear
    When his mother hovereth near,
And he hears her cheering call:
      "All-Aloney"?

Little All-Aloney's face
  It is all aglow with glee,
As around that romping-place
At a terrifying pace
  Lungeth, plungeth he!
And that hero seems to be
    All unconscious of our cheers—
    Only one dear voice he hears
Calling reassuringly:
      "All-Aloney!"

Though his legs bend with their load,
  Though his feet they seem so small
That you cannot help forebode
Some disastrous episode
  In that noisy hall,
Neither threatening bump nor fall
    Little All-Aloney fears,
    But with sweet bravado steers
Whither comes that cheery call:
      "All-Aloney!"

Ah, that in the years to come,
  When he shares of Sorrow's store,—
When his feet are chill and numb,
When his cross is burdensome,
  And his heart is sore:
Would that he could hear once more
  The gentle voice he used to hear—
  Divine with mother love and cheer—
Calling from yonder spirit shore:
      "All, all alone!"

THE CUNNIN' LITTLE THING

WHEN baby wakes of mornings,
    Then it's wake, ye people all!
      For another day
      Of song and play
Has come at our darling's call!
And, till she gets her dinner,
  She makes the welkin ring,
And she *won't* keep still till she's had her fill—
  The cunnin' little thing!

When baby goes a-walking,
  Oh, how her paddies fly!
      For that's the way
      The babies say
To other folk "by-by";
The trees bend down to kiss her,
  And the birds in rapture sing,
As there she stands and waves her hands—
  The cunnin' little thing!

When baby goes a-rocking
　In her bed at close of day,
　　At hide-and-seek
　　On her dainty cheek
　The dreams and the dimples play;
Then it's sleep in the tender kisses
　The guardian angels bring
From the Far Above to my sweetest love—
　You cunnin' little thing!

THE DOLL'S WOOING

THE little French doll was a dear little doll
　Tricked out in the sweetest of dresses;
　　Her eyes were of hue
　　A most delicate blue
And dark as the night were her tresses;
Her dear little mouth was fluted and red,
And this little French doll was so very well bred
That whenever accosted her little mouth said:
　　"Mamma! mamma!"

The stockinet doll, with one arm and one leg,
　Had once been a handsome young fellow,
　　But now he appeared
　　Rather frowzy and bleared
　In his torn regimentals of yellow;
Yet his heart gave a curious thump as he lay
In the little toy cart near the window one day
And heard the sweet voice of that French dolly say:
　　"Mamma! mamma!"

He listened so long and he listened so hard
  That anon he grew ever so tender,
      For it's everywhere known
      That the feminine tone
  Gets away with all masculine gender!
He up and he wooed her with soldierly zest,
But all she'd reply to the love he professed
Were *these* plaintive words (which perhaps you have
    guessed):
      "Mamma! mamma!"

Her mother—a sweet little lady of five—
  Vouchsafed her parental protection,
      And although stockinet
      Wasn't blue-blooded, yet
  She really could make no objection!
So soldier and dolly were wedded one day,
And a moment ago, as I journeyed that way,
I'm sure that I heard a wee baby voice say:
      "Mamma! mamma!"

INSCRIPTION FOR MY LITTLE
SON'S SILVER PLATE

WHEN thou dost eat from off this plate,
    I charge thee be thou temperate;
Unto thine elders at the board
Do thou sweet reverence accord;
And, though to dignity inclined,
Unto the serving-folk be kind;
Be ever mindful of the poor,
Nor turn them hungry from the door;
And unto God, for health and food
And all that in thy life is good,
Give thou thy heart in gratitude.

SEEIN' THINGS

I AIN'T afeard uv snakes, or toads, or bugs, or worms, or mice,
An' things 'at girls are skeered uv I think are awful nice!
I'm pretty brave, I guess; an' yet I hate to go to bed,
For, when I'm tucked up warm an' snug an' when my prayers are
    said,
Mother tells me "Happy dreams!" and takes away the light,
An' leaves me lyin' all alone an' seein' things at night!

Sometimes they're in the corner, sometimes they're by the door,
Sometimes they're all a-standin' in the middle uv the floor;
Sometimes they are a-sittin' down, sometimes they're walkin' round
So softly an' so creepylike they never make a sound!
Sometimes they are as black as ink, an' other times they're white—
But the color ain't no difference when you see things at night!

Once, when I licked a feller 'at had just moved on our street,
An' father sent me up to bed without a bite to eat,
I woke up in the dark an' saw things standin' in a row,
A-lookin' at me cross-eyed an' p'intin' at me—so!
Oh, my! I wuz so skeered that time I never slep' a mite—
It's almost alluz when I'm bad I see things at night!

Lucky thing I ain't a girl, or I'd be skeered to death!
Bein' I'm a boy, I duck my head an' hold my breath;
An' I am, oh! *so* sorry I'm a naughty boy, an' then
I promise to be better an' I say my prayers again!
Gran'ma tells me that's the only way to make it right
When a feller has been wicked an' sees things at night!

An' so, when other naughty boys would coax me into sin,
I try to skwush the Tempter's voice 'at urges me within;
An' when they's pie for supper, or cakes 'at's big an' nice,
I want to—but I do not pass my plate f'r them things twice!
No, ruther let Starvation wipe me slowly out o' sight
Than I should keep a-livin' on an' seein' things at night!

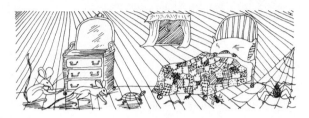

FISHERMAN JIM'S KIDS

FISHERMAN JIM lived on the hill
    With his bonnie wife an' his little boys;
'Twuz "Blow, ye winds, as blow ye will—
    Naught we reck of your cold and noise!"
        For happy and warm were he an' his,
And he dandled his kids upon his knee
To the song of the sea.

Fisherman Jim would sail all day,
    But, when come night, upon the sands
His little kids ran from their play,
    Callin' to him an' wavin' their hands;
        Though the wind was fresh and the sea was high,
He'd hear 'em—you bet—above the roar
Of the waves on the shore!

Once Fisherman Jim sailed into the bay
    As the sun went down in a cloudy sky,
And never a kid saw he at play,
    And he listened in vain for the welcoming cry.

In his little house he learned it all,
And he clinched his hands and he bowed his head—
"The fever!" they said.

'Twuz a pitiful time for Fisherman Jim,
   With them darlin's a-dyin afore his eyes,
A-stretçhin' their wee hands out to him
   An' a-breakin' his heart with the old-time cries
      He had heerd so often upon the sands;
For they thought they wuz helpin' his boat ashore—
Till they spoke no more.

But Fisherman Jim lived on and on,
   Castin' his nets an' sailin' the sea;
As a man will live when his heart is gone,
   Fisherman Jim lived hopelessly,
      Till once in those years they come an' said:
"Old Fisherman Jim is powerful sick—
Go to him, quick!"

Then Fisherman Jim says he to me:
   "It's a long, long cruise—you understand—
But over beyont the ragin' sea
   I kin see my boys on the shinin' sand
      Waitin' to help this ol' hulk ashore,
Just as they used to—ah, mate, you know!—
In the long ago."

No, sir! he wuzn't afeard to die,
   For all night long he seemed to see
His little boys of the days gone by.
      An' to hear sweet voices forgot by me!
      An' just as the mornin' sun come up—
"They're holdin' me by the hands!" he cried,
An' so he died.

"FIDDLE-DEE-DEE"

THERE once was a bird that lived up in a tree,
    And all he could whistle was "Fiddle-dee-dee"—
A very provoking, unmusical song
For one to be whistling the summer day long!
Yet always contented and busy was he
With that vocal recurrence of "Fiddle-dee-dee."

Hard by lived a brave little soldier of four,
That weird iteration repented him sore;
"I prithee, Dear-Mother-Mine! fetch me my gun,
For, by our St. Didy! the deed must be done
That shall presently rid all creation and me
Of that ominous bird and his 'Fiddle-dee-dee'!"

Then out came Dear-Mother-Mine, bringing her son
His awfully truculent little red gun;
The stock was of pine and the barrel of tin,
The "bang" it came out where the bullet went in—
The right kind of weapon I think you'll agree
For slaying all fowl that go "Fiddle-dee-dee"!

The brave little soldier quoth never a word,
But he up and he drew a straight bead on that bird;
And, while that vain creature provokingly sang,
The gun it went off with a terrible bang!
Then loud laughed the youth—"By my Bottle," cried he,
"I've put a quietus on 'Fiddle-dee-dee'!"

Out came then Dear-Mother-Mine, saying: "My son,
Right well have you wrought with your little red gun!
Hereafter no evil at all need I fear,
With such a brave soldier as You-My-Love here!"
She kissed the dear boy.
                  [The bird in the tree
Continued to whistle his "Fiddle-dee-dee"!]

OVER THE HILLS AND FAR AWAY

OVER the hills and far away,
  A little boy steals from his morning play,
And under the blossoming apple-tree
He lies and he dreams of the things to be:
Of battles fought and of victories won,
Of wrongs o'erthrown and of great deeds done—
Of the valor that he shall prove some day,
Over the hills and far away—
      Over the hills and far away!

Over the hills and far away
It's, oh, for the toil the livelong day!
But it mattereth not to the soul aflame
With a love for riches and power and fame!
On, O man! while the sun is high—
On to the certain joys that lie
Yonder where blazeth the noon of day,
Over the hills and far away—
      Over the hills and far away!

Over the hills and far away,
An old man lingers at close of day;
Now that his journey is almost done,
His battles fought and his victories won—
The old-time honesty and truth,
The trustfulness and the friends of youth,
Home and mother—where are they?
Over the hills and far away—
      Over the years and far away!

THE SONG OF LUDDY-DUD

A SUNBEAM comes a-creeping
    Into my dear one's nest,
And sings to our babe a-sleeping,
    The song that I love the best:
      " 'Tis little Luddy-Dud in the morning—
      'Tis little Luddy-Dud at night;
        And all day long
        'Tis the same sweet song
Of that waddling, toddling, coddling little mite,
    Luddy-Dud."

The bird to the tossing clover,
    The bee to the swaying bud,
Keeping singing that sweet song over
    Of wee little Luddy-Dud.
      " 'Tis little Luddy-Dud in the morning—
      'Tis little Luddy-Dud at night;
        And all day long
        'Tis the same dear song
Of that growing, crowing, knowing little sprite,
    Luddy-Dud!"

Luddy-Dud's cradle is swinging
    Where softly the night winds blow,
And Luddy-Dud's mother is singing
    A song that is sweet and low:
      " 'Tis little Luddy-Dud in the morning—
      'Tis little Luddy-Dud at night;
        And all day long
        'Tis the same sweet song
Of my nearest and my dearest heart's delight,
    Luddy-Dud!"